Coping with Behavioral Addictions

The Technology Addiction Workbook

Information, Assessments, and Tools for Managing Life with a Behavioral Addiction

Ester R.A. Leutenberg and John J. Liptak, EdD

Whole Person Associates
Mental Health & Wellness Publishers
Duluth, Minnesota

Whole Person Associates

101 West 2nd Street, Suite 203
Duluth, MN 55802-5004

800-247-6789

Books@WholePerson.com
WholePerson.com

The Technology Addiction Workbook

Editorial Director: Jack Kosmach
Art Director: Mathew Pawlak
Cover Design: Adam Sippola
Editor: Peg Johnson

Library of Congress Control Number: 2022949519
ISBN:978-1-57025-369-0

From the co-authors, Ester and John,
Our gratitude, thanks, and appreciation
to the following professionals:

☙ ○ ❧

Editorial Directors – Jack Kosmach and Peg Johnson

Editor and Lifelong Teacher – Eileen Regen, MEd, CIE

Reviewers – Niki Tilicki, MA Ed and Jay Leutenberg, CASA

Art Director – Mathew Pawlak

☙ ○ ❧

A Special Thank You
to
Whole Person Associates

for their interest in mental health issues.

Free PDF Download Available

To access your free PDF download of the assessment tools
and all of the reproducible activities in this workbook, go to:
https://WholePerson.com/store/TheTechnologyAddictionWorkbook9519.html

understanding Behavioral Addictions

There are many types of addictions. The behavioral addictions that are heard about most are substance abuse addictions. However, a behavioral addiction can be the same as a physical dependence on a substance.

> ...it is the compulsive nature of the behavior that is often indicative of a behavioral addiction, or process addiction, in an individual. The compulsion to continually engage in an activity or behavior despite the negative impact on the person's ability to remain mentally and/or physically healthy and functional in the home and community defines behavioral addiction. The person may find the behavior rewarding psychologically or get a "high" while engaged in the activity, but may later feel guilt, remorse, or even overwhelmed by the consequences of that continued choice. Unfortunately, as is common for all who struggle with addiction, people living with behavioral addictions are unable to stop engaging in the behavior for any length of time without treatment and intervention.

~ American Addiction Centers (2019)

People are increasingly experiencing non-substance behavioral addictions and diminished control over their behavior. Behavioral addictions are no longer categorized as impulse disorders, and behavioral addictions are now viewed as true addictions, much like substance abuse.

The National Institute of Health (2010) states:

> Growing evidence suggests that behavioral addictions resemble substance addictions in many domains, including natural history, phenomenology, tolerance, co-morbidity, overlapping genetic contribution, neurobiological mechanisms, and response to treatment.

~ Grant et al. 2010

The concept of addiction, for years adopted solely to indicate the use of psychotropic substances, is now being applied to describe a heterogeneous group of syndromes known as "behavioral addictions," "no-drug addictions," or "new addictions." Prevalence rates for such conditions, taken as a whole, are amongst the highest registered for mental disorders with social, cultural, and economic implications. Individual forms of behavioral addictions are linked by a series of psychopathological features that include repetitive, persistent, and dysfunctional behaviors, loss of control over behavior despite the negative repercussions of the latter, compulsion to satisfy the need to implement the behavior, initial well-being produced by the behavior, craving, onset of tolerance, abstinence and, ultimately, a progressive, significant impairment of overall individual functioning.

Why Are They Called Behavioral Addictions?

Behavioral addictions constitute any maladaptive pattern of excessive behavior that manifests in physiological, psychological, and cognitive symptoms such as the following:

- **Continuance:** continuing the behavior despite knowing that this activity is creating or exacerbating physical, psychological, or interpersonal problems.

- **Intention effects:** inability to stick to one's routine, as evidenced by exceeding the amount of time devoted to the behavior or consistently going beyond the intended amount.

- **Lack of control:** unsuccessful attempts to reduce the level of the behavior or cease it for a certain period of time.

- **Reduction in activities:** as a direct result of the behavior, social, familial, occupational, or recreational activities occur less often or are stopped.

- **Time:** a great deal of time is spent preparing for, engaging in, and recovering from the behavior.

- **Tolerance:** increasing the amount of the behavior to feel the desired effect, be it a "buzz" or a sense of accomplishment.

- **Withdrawal:** in the absence of the behavior, the person experiences adverse effects such as anxiety, irritability, restlessness, and sleep problems.

Addiction to Technology

Since the emergence of the internet and smartphones, an increasing number of people are struggling with an addiction to some form of technology. Constantly being plugged into a smartphone, social media, or other devices and being on the internet leads to fear of not hearing about activities and being left out of news and information. Given the neurological changes that occur while being online, more and more people are at risk of developing a technology addiction.

Technology addictions, also referred to as Information and Communication Technologies (ICTs) addiction, involve any form of human-technology interaction and can include passive (e.g., television), active (e.g., video games), or social (e.g., social media sites) interaction with technology, and usually contain inducing and reinforcing features which may contribute to the promotion of addictive tendencies. According to Deyan Georgiev (2022):

- Most mobile phone users check their phones up to 63 times daily.
- Americans spend an average screen time of 5.4 hours on their mobile phones daily.
- There will be over 311.53 million smartphone users in America by 2025.
- Social media accounts for 2.5 hours of global internet time spent online by an average user daily.
- 13% of millennials spend over 12 hours on their phones daily.
- Baby Boomers spend 5 hours using their phones.
- Millennials spend 48 minutes texting every day.

The significant factors that foster an addiction to technology include the ability to get in touch with other people quickly and easily, accessibility, availability, intimacy, high stimulation, and anonymity. Most technological addictions involve using TV, the internet, smartphones, video game consoles, and other devices. However, the accessibility of new technologies, like social media sites, which have the advantages of portability and an ever-growing array of social functions, makes their overuse increasingly likely.

TECHNOLOGY ADDICTION IN THE DSM-5

Although absent from the present diagnostic guidelines, such as the World Health Organization's 2018 International Classification of Diseases (ICD) and the Diagnostic and American Psychiatric Association's 2018 Statistical Manual of Mental Disorders (DSM-5), experts have recognized that the use of technology can quickly and easily become an addiction and lead to physical, occupational, social, and psychological problems.

Proposed diagnostic criteria for a technology addiction (the abuse of the internet, social media, mobile phones, and video games) include the following:
1) tolerance or the need for increased use of the technologies over time
2) withdrawal or emotionally intense discomfort when spending an unusual length of time without using the technology or when use is disrupted
3) greater use than intended when beginning a session
4) desire to stop the use of the technology without being able to do so
5) spending too much time engaged in activities related to the technologies
6) stopping other offline activities to increase the use of the internet, mobile phones, or video games
7) continued use of the internet, mobile phones, or video games despite an awareness that such use is causing damage to personal relationships and professional ambitions.

The overuse and over-dependence on technology can be a behavioral addiction that can be effectively treated using a range of cognitive and behavioral therapies.

Signs of Potential Technology Addiction

Addiction to technology suggests the overuse of any technology that disrupts various aspects of life. As the intensity of technology use increases, the person is at risk of becoming addicted to it. However, it is possible that a person can have a technology addiction without being totally out of control.

Signs of a Person at Risk

People with an addiction to technology may ...

- Compulsively check text messages, change their social media status, and upload selfies.
- Feel euphoric while on the web and restless, moody, depressed, or irritable when attempting to control technology use.
- Withdraw from social activities.
- Lose interest in activities that do not involve a computer, phone, or gadget.
- Experience feelings of restlessness when unable to go online.
- Use the phone or attempt to keep it on even when asked to turn it off.
- Use online interactions through social media as a primary way to communicate with others.
- Feel uncomfortable or agitated without technology, even for a brief time.
- Be unable to function without using technology, even for a brief period.
- Resort to extreme measures to maintain connections with their technology.
- Find their friends and family members expressing concern about the level of technology use.
- Fail at efforts to control, cut back, or stop technology use.
- Jeopardize a significant relationship, job, educational, or career opportunity.
- Lie to family members or others to conceal their involvement with various technologies.
- Use technology to escape from problems.
- Use technology in dangerous situations.
- Experience harm or repeated interruptions to social life, family life, and physical and mental well-being.
- Experience urges to repeat the behavior.
- Demonstrate dependence, tolerance, and increasing need for stimulation to achieve satisfaction.
- Display anxiety or negative feelings associated with the inability to send or receive immediate responses.
- Allow technology use to be very time-consuming.
- Experience distress when technology fails or is not available.
- Increase levels of smartphone use to the point that friends and family members express concern.

Risk Factors

Excessive technology use can include the following issues:

- Lifestyle Issues: More time spent with technology allows less time for a balanced lifestyle. This can lead to various physical consequences such as eyestrain, blurred vision, headaches, pain and strain from habitually unhealthy posture, and susceptibility to accidents while carrying out other tasks (walking, biking, driving). It can increase familial, occupational, and financial problems.
- Social Development Issues: As more time is spent online rather than face-to-face interaction, social skill development may be hindered and eventually lead to social withdrawal.
- Sleep Deprivation Issues: Using devices may cut into sleep cycles, and the individual may feel wired and unable to rest well.
- Psychological Issues: Excessive use of technology is associated with several mental health concerns, such as poor psychological well-being, a lack of self-confidence, anxiety, sadness, lower social and emotional intelligence, and lower overall life and job satisfaction.

Some Types of Addictive Technology

People become addicted to technology through many different avenues. They can include the following:

The internet. The internet can be addictive as a multifunctional tool that brings people enormous amounts of information in record time. As the internet has become increasingly more accessible, people have access on computers, tablets, phones, and watches.

Video and computer games. A video game is any electronic game that involves interaction with a user interface to generate visual feedback on two- or three-dimensional video display devices such as a TV screen, virtual reality headset, or computer monitor. Like the internet, video games have become increasingly accessible to people through consoles, computers, tablets, and phones.

Smartphones, tablets, and lifestyle technologies. Mobile phones have the power to keep people constantly connected. Smartphones, tablets, and the emergence of other smart devices, including smart watches, smart speakers, or devices connected to voice-controlled virtual assistance services: these technologies promote addiction by removing the time it takes a person to complete tasks and activities that previously required logging onto a desktop or laptop computer.

Social media. Social media provides individually-relevant information through centralized, personalized portals, such as Facebook newsfeeds, Twitter accounts, LinkedIn articles, blogs, YouTube subscriptions, or TikTok followership. No matter how carefully we list technology, we will always fall short. New technologies such as robotics, artificial intelligence, and AR/VR will continue to expand.

What Makes Technology Addictive?

Technology is addictive primarily because it fulfills our natural human need for interaction, stimulation, and life changes with great efficiency. Thus, technology can become a quick and easy way to fill a person's basic needs. When used this way, it can become addictive. Technology impacts the pleasure systems of the brain in ways similar to substances. Like substances, it can help overcome boredom, be a social outlet, and provide an escape from the reality of everyday life. Video and computer games, smartphones and tablets, social media, and the internet provide a variety of ways to access the power and appeal of technology that can promote dependence on this technology:

- Technology can be used to alleviate anxiety and sadness.

- Technology can be an escape from reality and offers the chance to assume new identities that are more appealing than a person's own identity in real life.

- Technology can fulfill a person's need for social connection and allow endless online relationships without typical boundaries of time and geography.

- Technology provides a sense of control and autonomy for people who feel their lives are out of control.

- Technology provides links for people to share their hobbies and interests.

- Technology helps people to feel competent, autonomous, and connected to other people.

- Technology allows people to stay connected so they aren't the last to know about a news story or social event.

Using This Workbook

The Technology Addiction Workbook provides helping professionals with cognitive and behavioral assessments, tools, and exercises that can be utilized to treat the root psychological causes of technology addiction. It is designed to help people identify and change unhealthy thoughts and behaviors that may have led to technology addiction. The activities in this workbook can help participants identify the triggers that can lead to the overuse of technology and teach them ways to overcome and manage those triggers.

The Technology Addiction Workbook will help participants to achieve the following:

- Recognize that they are experiencing an addiction problem.
- Reflect upon the behaviors that are part of and arose from the addiction.
- Build self-esteem in positive capabilities outside the use of technology.
- Understand the triggers for preoccupation with various aspects of technology.
- Develop greater self-acceptance and the ability to change ineffective behaviors.
- Understand recurring patterns that indicate a technology addiction.
- Learn ways to live a new life without obsessing over technology.

The Technology Addiction Workbook is a practical tool for teachers, counselors, and helping professionals in their work with people suffering from behavioral addictions. Depending on the role of the person using this workbook and the specific group's or individual's needs, the modules can be used individually or as part of an integrated curriculum. The facilitator can administer an activity with a group or individual or use multiple assessments in a workshop.

Confidentiality When Completing Activity Handouts

Participants will see the words **NAME CODES** on some of the activities in the modules. Instruct participants that when writing or speaking about anyone, they should use name codes for people to preserve privacy and anonymity. Using these codes will allow participants to explore their feelings without hurting anyone's feelings or fearing gossip, harm, or retribution. For example, a friend named Sherry, who **R**eads **M**any **B**ooks might be assigned a **NAME CODE** of **RMB** for a particular exercise. To protect others' identities, they will not use people's actual names or initials, only **NAME CODES**.

The Five Modules

The Technology Addiction Workbook contains five modules of activity-based handouts that will help participants learn more about themselves and their technology addiction. These modules serve as avenues for self-reflection and group experiences revolving around topics of importance in the participants' lives.

The activities in this workbook are user-friendly and varied to provide a comprehensive way of analyzing, strengthening, and developing characteristics, skills, and attitudes for overcoming an addiction to technology.

The activities and handouts in this workbook are reproducible. Minor revisions to suit client or group needs are permitted, but the copyright statement must be retained.

Module 1: Cultivating Awareness

This module helps participants explore how their overuse (often addiction) of technology affects their lives, examine problems caused by the overuse of technology, learn ways to become more mindful, become aware of the physical symptoms of technology overuse, and recognize and effectively deal with technology triggers.

Module 2: Digital Well-Being

This module helps participants explore how overuse and overdependence on technology can interfere with their general well-being. They will examine how the overuse of technology can be destructive in various ways, and they will learn how to make lifestyle changes to alter the ways and the amount of time they spend using technology.

Module 3: Unplugging

This module helps participants examine how much they are overusing technology, the intensity of their addiction, and ways to unplug and start reconnecting with themselves more holistically. They will explore what they miss because they are overusing technology and learn ways to unplug.

Module 4: Finding Balance

This module helps participants focus on how much time they spend with the major technology types. They will examine ways to get the same benefits from engaging in other activities, determine methods for balancing technology and relationships, explore how to balance technology and work, and define ways to engage other people in their lives as they begin disconnecting from their overuse of technology.

Module 5: Technology Overuse

This module helps participants discover how they may be overusing technology to mask challenges and escape the reality of their problems. They will find ways of coping with stress other than using technology, think more clearly, connect with people offline, and engage in non-technology leisure activities.

Different Types of Activity Handouts Included in This Workbook

A variety of materials are included in this reproducible workbook:

- **Action Plans** that assist participants in meeting the goals and objectives of treatment.

- **Assessments** that allow participants to explore their behavior. They can be used again to allow participants to track their progress.

- **Drawing and Doodling** allow participants to unleash the power of the right side of the brain.

- **Educational Pages** that provide insights and tips related to the topic.

- **Group Activities** to encourage collaboration among participants.

- **Journaling Activities** can help participants clarify their thoughts and feelings, thus gaining helpful self-knowledge.

- **Positive Affirmations** allow participants to create formidable affirmations they can post and repeat to themselves when impulses begin.

- **Quotation Pages** allow participants to reflect on many powerful quotes and determine how they apply to their lives.

- **Tables** that require participants to reflect on their lives in the past, understand themselves in the present, and react more effectively in the future.

References

American Addiction Centers (2019). Behavioral Addictions.
https://americanaddictioncenters.org/behavioral-addictions

American Psychiatric Association (2018). Diagnostic and Statistical Manual of Mental Disorders (DSM–5),
https://www.psychiatry.org/psychiatrists/practice/dsm

Georgiev, D. (2022). How much time does the average American spend on their phone in 2022? Oct 13, 2022.
https://techjury.net/blog/how-much-time-does-the-average-american-spend-on-their-phone/

National Institute of Health (2010). Introduction to Behavioral Addictions.
https://www.ncbi.nlm.nih.gov/pmc/articles/PMC3164585

World Health Organization (2018). International Classification of Diseases (ICD) Information Sheet.
https://www.who.int/classifications/icd/factsheet/en/

Table of Contents

Introduction – The Technology Addiction Workbook iii
    Understanding Behavioral Addictions...iv
    Why Are They Called Behavioral Addictions?.. v
    Addiction to Technology and Technology Addiction in the DSM-5...........................vi
    Signs of Potential Technology Addiction... vii
    Risk Factors and Some Types of Addictive Technology........................... viii
    What Makes Technology Addictive ix
    Using this Workbook and Confidentiality When Completing Activity Handouts x
    The Five Modules xi
    Different Types of Activity Handouts Included in this Workbook and References.............. xii
    Table of Contents .... xiii-xv

Module 1 – Cultivating Awareness 17
    Cultivating Awareness Assessment Introduction and Directions 19
    Cultivating Awareness Assessment (Page 1)..20
    Cultivating Awareness Assessment (Page 2) and Scoring Directions 21
    Cultivating Awareness Assessment Scale Descriptions and Profile Interpretation 22
    My Current Technology Usage...23
    Distracted by Technology 24
    Fear of Missing Out (FOMO)...25
    Problems, Problems, and More Problems...26
    What Are You Escaping From? 27
    Changed Relationship Warning Signs..28
    General Warning Signs..29
    Physical Symptoms 30
    Be Aware!...31
    Attempts to Unplug 32
    Increasing Amounts...33
    What Happens When I Cut Back?..34
    Constantly Checking 35
    The Virtual and Real Worlds 36
    Quotes about Overuse of Technology...37

(Continued on page xiv)

Table of Contents

Module 2 – Digital Well-Being 39
    Digital Well-Being Assessment Introduction and Directions 41
    Digital Well-Being Assessment 42
    Digital Well-Being Assessment Scoring Descriptions and Profile Interpretation 43
    Positive Effects of Technology 44
    Destructive Effects of Technology 45
    Safe Driving. 46
    Two Types of Interaction. 47
    Technology Autopilot 48
    The Dark Side of Technology 49
    Create Boundaries for Yourself. 50
    Recharging 51
    Make Adjustments to Your Devices and Yourself. 52
    Single-Tasking 53
    Unplugging 54
    Device-Free Zones and Times 55
    Wind Down for a Better Night's Sleep 56
    Time Without Screens 57
    Creating Connection 58
    Quotes about Digital Well-Being. 59

Module 3 – Unplugging 61
    Technology Intensity Assessment Introduction and Directions 63
    Technology Intensity Assessment 64
    Technology Intensity Assessment Scoring Descriptions and Profile Interpretation 65
    Reconnect with Myself. 66
    Benefits of Unplugging. 67
    Mindful Eating 68
    Relaxation 69
    What Am I Missing?. 70
    When I Unplug Some of the Time. 71
    Time to Reconnect 72
    Unplugging at Night. 73
    Meditation in the Morning 74
    Write a Letter or Thank You Note 75
    Leave Work at Work 76
    Become More Active 77
    Do Something for Others. 78
    I Might Miss Out!. 79
    Do More Things Offline 80
    Quotes about Unplugging From Technology 81

(Continued on page xv)

Table of Contents

Module 4 – Finding Balance..83
    Technology Assessment Introduction and Directions....................................85
    Technology Assessment (Page 1)...86
    Technology Assessment (Page 2)...87
    Technology Assessment Scoring Descriptions and Profile Interpretation...........88
    How about Offline Highs?...89
    I'm Tired...90
    Being Out of Balance..91
    Am I Disconnected?..92
    Balancing Relationships...93
    Work-Life Balance...94
    Loneliness...95
    Won't You Be My Neighbor?...96
    Human Interactions..97
    "I've Been Meaning To…"...98
    Living Out of Balance...99
    Out of Balance?..100
    Go Outside...101
    Rediscover Technology Alternatives..102
    Break Up with the Level of Your Technology..103
    Quotes about Balancing Life and Technology...104

Module 5 – Technology Overuse...105
    Technology Overuse Assessment Introduction and Directions.............................107
    Technology Overuse Assessment...108
    Technology Overuse Assessment Scoring Descriptions and Profile Interpretation.......109
    Coping with Stress (Page 1)...110
    Coping with Stress (Page 2)...111
    Think More Realistically..112
    Connected Online and Offline..113
    Thinking Like a Victim..114
    Automatic Responses (Page 1)..115
    Automatic Responses (Page 2)..116
    Automatic Responses (Page 3)..117
    Your Stories about Unplugging...118
    No-Tech Leisure...119
    Join Something..120
    Habits..121
    Making New Friends..122
    Justifications..123
    I'm Afraid of Rejection...124
    Keep Me on Track..125
    Need to Change Your Tech Habits?..126
    Quotes about Technology Overuse...127

Technology

Cultivating Awareness

Name _____

Date _____

Cultivating Awareness Assessment
Introduction and Directions

Technology is a wonderful thing. Whether using your smartphone to find your way to a new restaurant, using social media to keep up with current trends, or texting your family to let them know you are safe, technology is very helpful. However, it can become a problem and even an addiction when you overuse it.

The *Cultivating Awareness Assessment* is designed to help you become aware of whether you are overly dependent on your technology. It contains statements that are divided into five categories.

Read each statement and decide how descriptive it is of you. For each of the choices listed, circle the number of your response on the line to the right of each statement.

In the following example, the circled 2 indicates the statement is LIKE the person completing the inventory:

                                                              LIKE ME   UNLIKE ME

I.   Related to my technology use ...

I constantly check my text messages no matter what I am doing . . . . (2) 1

I constantly check my text messages no matter where I am . . . . (2) 1

This is not a test. Since there are no right or wrong answers, do not spend too much time thinking about your answers. Be sure to respond to every statement. The purpose of this assessment is for YOU to learn more about YOU and your technology habits.

BE HONEST!

If you choose, no one else needs to see the results.

(Turn to the next page and begin.)

Cultivating Awareness Assessment (Page 1)

Name _____ Date _____

This will only be accurate if you respond honestly. No one else needs to see this if you choose.

                                                                    LIKE ME   UNLIKE ME

I.   Related to my technology use ...

I constantly check my text messages no matter what I am doing 2 1
I constantly check my text messages no matter where I am 2 1
I check social media sites numerous times a day to keep up to date 2 1
I take selfies continually 2 1
I check my status on social media sites at every opportunity 2 1
I check likes, dislikes, and comments to my posts all day long 2 1

Preoccupation TOTAL = _____

                                                                    LIKE ME   UNLIKE ME

II.   Related to my technology use ...

I have a feeling of euphoria while using technology 2 1
I constantly feel the urge to use technology 2 1
I am irritable when I cannot access technology 2 1
I put work-school at risk because of prioritizing my technology use 2 1
I know that I am obsessed with checking my phone 2 1
I can't imagine life without technology 2 1

Not Using TOTAL = _____

                                                                    LIKE ME   UNLIKE ME

III. Related to my technology use ...

I have tried to use technology less 2 1
I find myself withdrawing from face-to-face interactions with people 2 1
I am not interested in any non-technology-based activities 2 1
I will use technology even when I don't need to 2 1
I need the stimulation of clicking "send" to feel satisfied 2 1
I have an increasing need to use my technology more 2 1

Withdrawing TOTAL = _____

(Continued on the next page.)

Cultivating Awareness Assessment (Page 2)

Name _____ Date _____

This will only be accurate if you respond honestly. No one else needs to see this if you choose.

                                                                    LIKE ME   UNLIKE ME

IV.   Related to my technology use ...

I will go to extreme measures to stay connected 2 1

I use technology in dangerous situations 2 1

I have lied to others to conceal my usage 2 1

Others have expressed concerns about my usage 2 1

I can't wait for my next online session or activity 2 1

I use it to escape from the reality of my problems 2 1

Extremes TOTAL = _____

                                                                    LIKE ME   UNLIKE ME

V.   Related to my technology use ...

I have ruined relationships because of my use of technology 2 1

I have harmed my work-school situation 2 1

I routinely stay online for excessively long periods 2 1

I have started to cut back on sleep to stay connected 2 1

I am neglecting family and friends because of my use of technology 2 1

I don't care about anything except my smartphone 2 1

Harm TOTAL = _____

Scoring Directions

The *Cultivating Awareness Assessment* is designed to measure the nature of your addiction and the severity of your technology addiction.

For each of the five sections of the assessment on the previous pages, count the scores you circled for each of the six items, and put that total on the line marked TOTAL at the end of each section. Then, transfer your totals to the spaces below:

I.	**Preoccupation Total**	=	_____
II.	**Not Using Total**	=	_____
III.	**Withdrawing Total**	=	_____
IV.	**Extremes Total**	=	_____
V.	**Harm Total**	=	_____

Cultivating Awareness Assessment

Scale Descriptions and Profile Interpretation

For each section, place an X on the line to note your scores from the previous page.

SCALE 1 – Preoccupation

This scale measures how much time you spend thinking about and using technology.

6 = Low	9 = Moderate	12 = High

SCALE 2 – Not Using

This scale measures your dependence on technology and the extent of your being upset when unable to use it.

6 = Low	9 = Moderate	12 = High

SCALE 3 – Withdrawing

This scale measures how much you need to increase, rather than decrease, your technology use.

6 = Low	9 = Moderate	12 = High

SCALE 4 – Extremes

This scale measures how far you will go to overuse technology, even if your usage is becoming a problem.

6 = Low	9 = Moderate	12 = High

SCALE 5 – Harm

This scale measures how much technology has negatively affected your life due to its overuse.

6 = Low	9 = Moderate	12 = High

Remember that one high score on any scale can suggest you are experiencing a problem overusing technology. The HIGHER your score on each of the scales of the Cultivating Awareness Assessment, the more of a problem you have with technology in the specific aspect measured by the assessment. Areas where you scored low suggest that you are not experiencing many signs of technology addiction in those areas, but even anything above a six score can suggest that it could be a problem.

My Current Technology Usage

It is important to start tracking your technology habit. Use the form below to track your technology usage.

When using this form, choose a day on which you would like to track your technology use and record it in the spaces that follow. Ideally, doing this every day might be enlightening.

DAY: _____

My Technology	Times Accessed	Why Checked
Email		
Internet Surfing		
Social Media Sites		
Smartphone Usage		
Texts		
Video Games		
Other		
Other		

Distracted by Technology

It might be shocking to see and acknowledge the number of times you have been distracted by technology, only to miss out on something in your environment, to be put in harm's way, or miss out on meaningful personal and professional opportunities. With awareness comes the ability to change your present activities and thus your behavior.

In the spaces that follow, explore the times you were distracted by some type of technology use and the outcome of the experience.

Times I Was Distracted	What Was Occurring	The Outcome
Example: In class, when the teacher talked about a scholarship.	*I was looking at my phone and missed the information.*	*I didn't get the scholarship, which would have helped me pay for college.*

I attribute much of my success in New York to my ability
to understand and avoid unnecessary distractions.
~ Derek Jeters

Fear of Missing Out (FOMO)

FOMO, the fear of missing out, suggests a lack of engagement with life. People who use technology excessively may need to constantly catch up, keep up, and measure up to others technologically.

In the left column, write what you are afraid of missing out on. In the right column, elaborate on your fear and write about why you feel this way.

Game Release Announcement	*I'm afraid of missing notification for video game releases.* *I need to be the first in my gaming group to know.*

Mindfulness Technique

Mindfulness is being able to identify your thoughts, feelings, and environment. It is looking at life rather than a screen. It is becoming more mindful of what you are doing in the present moment. Rather than drifting off into autopilot with some technology, take note of everything happening around you. The next time you go somewhere, notice every sign you pass, buildings you see, the beauty of nature around you, people's faces and body language, pets taking a walk, the length of the grass, the type of flowers that are blooming.

Problems, Problems, and More Problems

Technology can cause problems in many aspects of your life. Problems with technology use can often show up in a job (getting fired), education (can't keep up with studies), or career (too busy gaming to seek a promotion).

Think about problems you are experiencing in these three areas and describe them below. Explore how to reduce excessive technology use to become more effective in these areas.

Areas	Problems Due to Technology Overuse	How I Can Reduce the Overuse and Become More Effective
Job		
Education		
Career		

We are living in dystopia, in a world that is dominated by technology and disconnect, alienation, loneliness, and dysfunction.
~ Steven Wilson

What Are You Escaping From?

Many people overuse technology to escape feelings of sadness, loneliness, helplessness, constant anxiety, shame, guilt, etc.

Below write, draw, or doodle six things you try to escape from by overusing technology.

1.	2.
3.	4.
5.	6.

Changed Relationship Warning Signs

You have probably overlooked or ignored many warning signs of problems in your relationships, which are caused by you and your overuse of technology. Any addiction can create problems and be the reason for negative changes in relationships.

Because of technology, you may have the following relationship problems ...
- Jeopardized or risked the loss of a partner.
- Lost friends who are tired of you always having your head in technology equipment.
- Used technology as a way of escaping from family problems or people who bully.
- Become defensive when confronted by family members about the behavior.
- Lied to family members or friends to conceal the extent of your involvement with technology.

On the top boxes, identify three relationships that have negatively changed due to your technology addiction. Explain how your technology use might have been the issue, and how you can recover these relationships. On the bottom boxes, identify three relationships that seem to be negatively changing. Explain how your technology use might be an issue, and how you can be sure these relationships will not change in a negative way.

Relationships That Have Negatively Changed (USE NAME CODES)	How My Technology Use Might Have Been the Issue	How I Can Recover These Relationships

Relationships That Seem to Be Negatively Changing (USE NAME CODES)	How My Technology Use Might Be an Issue	How I Can Be Sure These Relationships Will Not Negatively Change

General Warning Signs

To overcome an addiction to technology, watch for warning signs.

For each warning sign in the first column below, describe how you noticed that warning sign and how you can use it to recover.

Warning Signs	How I Noticed These Signs And with Whom? (USE NAME CODES)	How I Can Use These Signs to Recover
Example: Experiencing a Sense of Euphoria While Plugged In	*I was gaming with friends for 5 hours, feeling zoned out, and forgot to eat dinner.*	*I will set a timer for dinner time and limit my gaming time to 3 hours.*
Experiencing a Sense of Euphoria While Plugged In		
Neglecting Friends and Family		
Skimping on Sleep		
Lying about Usage		
Feeling Ashamed, Guilty, or Depressed as a Result of Neglecting People and Life Events		
Feeling Anxiety or Sadness When Not Using Technology		
Withdrawing from Other Activities that Were Once Pleasurable		
Other		

Physical Symptoms

Most people experience many different types of physical symptoms from their addiction. Physical symptoms of technology addiction often include weight gain or weight loss, carpal tunnel syndrome, headaches, neck problems, backaches, dry red eyes, etc.

In the circles below, describe some physical symptoms you have experienced. In the space next to the symptoms, describe how you can reduce them.

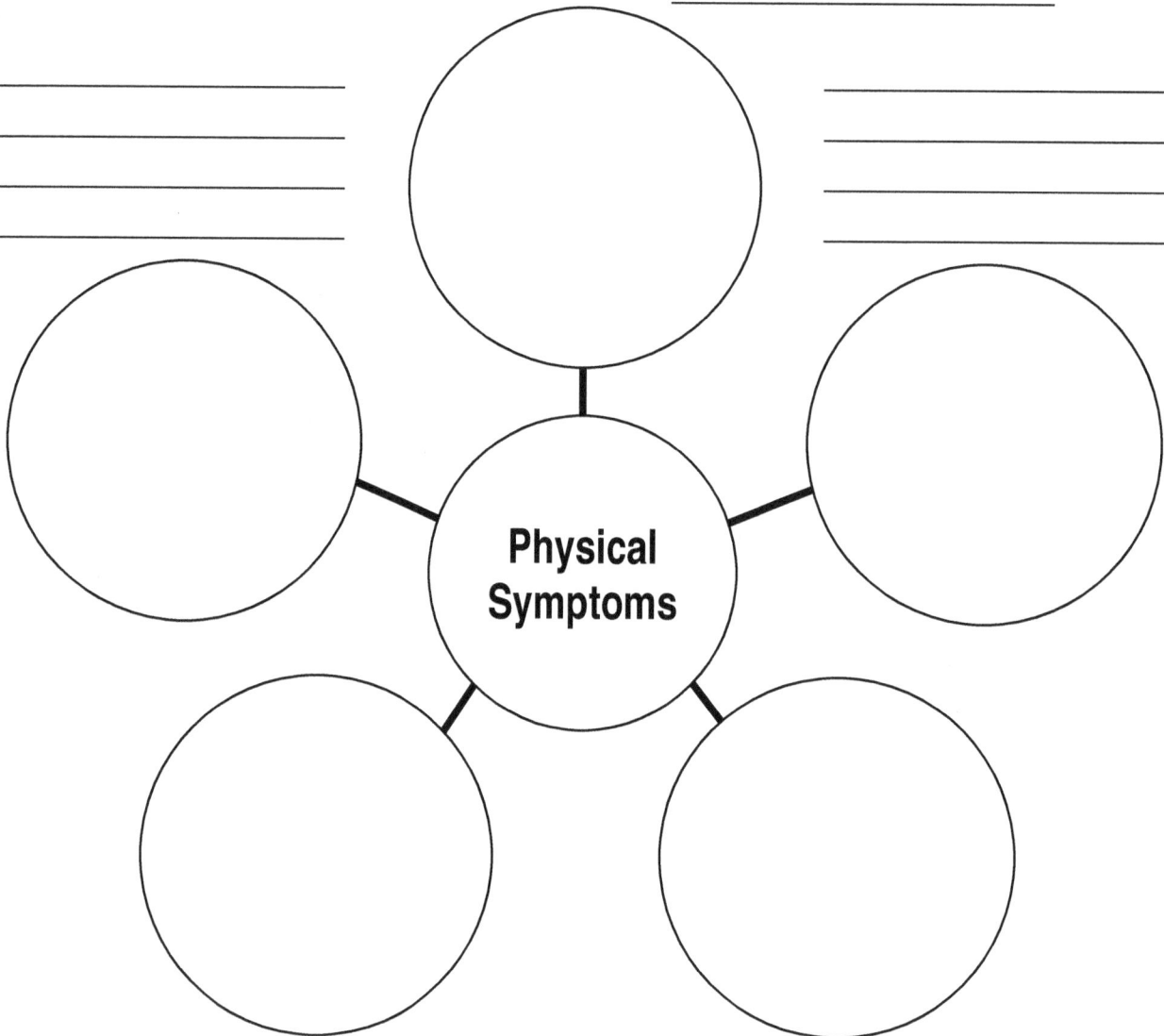

Physical Symptoms

Be Aware!

Social media sites, cell phone providers, and browsers will do everything possible to keep you addicted. Some rewards "games" go something like this:

- They provide free apps to access more information.
- The more you engage, the more data you can access.
- Pop-ups intrigue you to search more and buy more.
- You are made to feel as if you are missing out if you do not engage.

Below, explore some of the ways that apps or games have powered or increased your addiction.

Apps That Engage Me	How They Engage Me	Ways I Can Break Free
Example: A free app to access health information about yourself.	*Provided the app on my phone when I purchased the phone.*	*Delete apps that are not critical to my well-being.*

Below, journal about how people in your support system help you fight these temptations. How can you ask them for help?

_____

_____

_____

_____

Attempts to Unplug

You may have tried to unplug and cut back from your use of technology. Describe your attempts to control, cut back, or stop using technology as much.

My Attempt to Control, Cut Back, or Stop	Type of Technology (Phone, Internet, etc.)	Result or Outcome	What Can I Do Next?
Example: I have declared one day per week a "social media free" day.	Social media sites, including Facebook and Twitter.	I don't use social media. I feel much less stressed on those days.	Increase the number of social media free days to two per week.
Example: I started turning off my technology at 10:00 pm every night.	My computer and cell phone.	I am sleeping much better at night.	I can lower the time I turn off my technology to 9:00 pm.

I find it refreshing to unplug from it for a while.
You kind of forget how deeply you get embedded in it.
~ Will Wright

What is your reaction to Will Wright's quotation? _____

_____

_____

Increasing Amounts

People addicted to technology can't seem to get enough of it. They become preoccupied with it and think about their previous online activity or anticipate the next session. They need to use technology for increasing amounts of time to achieve satisfaction and often stay online longer than intended.

Complete each of the following statements.

When I am not using technology, I feel ...

_____

_____

When I am using technology, I ...

_____

_____

I often think about my last use of technology when ...

_____

_____

I am preoccupied with the following types of technology ...

_____

_____

I often lose a sense of time when I'm ...

_____

_____

I need to keep using technology more and more because ...

_____

_____

When I'm using technology, I am ...

_____

_____

What Happens When I Cut Back?

People with an addiction often feel restless, moody, depressed, or irritable with any attempt to cut back or stop.

Think about the times you have tried to stop or cut back, and describe the results of your attempts to reduce technology time.

Attempts to Cut Back	Results of My Attempt
Example: I tried to check my texts only three times during the day.	*I was able to accomplish this, then tried to limit it to one time per day, but I was unsuccessful.*

In this media-drenched, multitasking, always-on age, many of us have forgotten how to unplug and immerse ourselves completely in the moment. We have forgotten how to slow down. Not surprisingly, this fast-forward culture is taking a toll on everything from our diet and health to our work and the environment.
~ Carl Honore

What are your thoughts or feelings about the above quotation?

_____

_____

_____

_____

Constantly Checking

People who overuse technology obsessively check their devices. They need to respond immediately to a message, constantly check their phone even when it does not ring or vibrate, browse the internet just for something to do, check social media sites to see what their friends are doing, etc. They feel extremely anxious when they are away from their phone, device, or computer.

What are you constantly checking? Describe those experiences in the hexagons below:

Constantly Checking

The Virtual and Real Worlds

Many people who use technology enjoy living in a virtual world more than in the real world. In the virtual world, they have access to instant information, large amounts of data, and access to online connections, and social meeting places.

Describe how you favor what's happening in the virtual world and ignore what is happening in real time.

My Virtual World	My Real World
Example: I lost track of time while playing chess online.	*I missed my daughter's soccer game.*

How can you better balance your virtual and real worlds? _____

_____

_____

_____

_____

Quotes about Overuse of Technology

*On the lines that follow each of the quotes, describe how the
quote applies to your life and your current use of technology.*

I look at the way that my kids interact with technology, and it becomes a
mirror to the ways in which I myself interact with technology. I can see the
ways in which that addiction and compulsion starts to settle in on them,
and it's much more unnerving to see it in them than it is to experience it myself.
~ Franklin Foer

_____

_____

For the self-conscious or insecure girl, technology can become
a crippling addiction, an insatiable hunger not just for
connection but the elusive promise of being liked by everyone.
~ Rachel Simmons

_____

_____

It has become appallingly obvious that our technology has exceeded our humanity.
~ Albert Einstein

_____

_____

Sometimes you have to disconnect to stay connected. Remember the old days
when you had eye contact during a conversation? When everyone wasn't
looking down at a device in their hands? We've become so focused on that
tiny screen that we forget the big picture, the people right in front of us.
~ Regina Brett

_____

_____

Which quote especially speaks to you about your current use of technology? Why?

_____

_____

_____

_____

Technology

Digital Well-Being

Name _____

Date _____

Digital Well-Being Assessment
Introduction and Directions

As technology becomes more and more common and important in our lives, it can distract us from the things that matter most to us. When this occurs, overuse and overdependence on technology can interfere with our general well-being.

The *Digital Well-Being Assessment* contains 20 statements related to the use and overuse of technology on a daily basis. It can help you gauge whether technology is becoming a problem for you.

Read each of the statements and decide whether or not it describes you. If it does, circle the number in the TRUE column next to that item. If the statement does not describe you, circle the number in the NOT TRUE column next to that item.

In the following example, the circled 1 in the NOT TRUE column indicates that the person completing this assessment does __not__ believe that the statement describes them:

	TRUE	NOT TRUE

When it comes to the use of technology ...

I am not interacting as much with people face-to-face . . . . 2 . . . . (1)

I am experiencing back and neck aches. . . . . 2 . . . . (1)

This is not a test. Since there are no right or wrong answers, do not spend too much time thinking about your answers. Be sure to respond to every statement. The purpose of this assessment is for YOU to learn more about YOU and your technology habits.

BE HONEST!

If you choose, no one else needs to see the results.

(Turn to the next page and begin.)

Digital Well-Being Assessment

Name _____ Date _____

This will only be accurate if you respond honestly. No one else needs to see this if you choose.

	TRUE	NOT TRUE

When it comes to the use of technology ...

I am not interacting as much with people face-to-face .2 1

I am experiencing back and neck aches. 2 1

I don't get enough sleep. 2 1

I have used technology in dangerous situations like driving 2 1

I don't feel as connected with people in my life 2 1

I tend to access technology without even thinking. 2 1

I become distraught if my technology is not working .2 1

I text from anywhere, whether it's annoying to other people or not. 2 1

I become worried if I don't get an immediate response 2 1

I feel as if technology runs my life 2 1

I communicate better with people on social media than in person 2 1

I get upset if someone tries to limit the use of my cell phone. 2 1

I know that I am dependent on technology 2 1

I become furious if anyone suggests that I am overusing technology 2 1

I compulsively check emails. 2 1

I am probably obsessed with technology, but that's okay with me. 2 1

I hate when I am in a situation where I cannot use my cell phone 2 1

I completely lose track of time when I am using technology. 2 1

I cannot cut back on technology even when I try to 2 1

I use technology for longer periods of time. 2 1

Digital Well-Being TOTAL = _____

Go to the next page for scoring assessment results, profile interpretation, and individual description.

Digital Well-Being Assessment

Scoring Descriptions and Profile Interpretation

The assessment you just completed is designed to measure your awareness of the impact of technology on your life. Count the scores you circled. Enter that number on the total line. Then, transfer your total to the space below:

Digital Well-Being TOTAL = _____

Assessment Profile Interpretation

By circling even ONE TRUE answer, you could be at risk of developing or having a technology addiction. The more TRUE answers you circled, the greater the risk of experiencing a problem with your use of technology. The HIGHER your score on the *Digital Well-Being Assessment*, the more of an issue you have due to the overuse of technology.

20 = Low	**30 = Moderate**	**40 = High**

What is your reaction to your score? Were you honest?

_____

_____

_____

_____

_____

_____

Positive Effects of Technology

It is important to learn to balance your use of technology and other areas of your life to maintain stability and overall well-being. The positive use of technology affects many aspects of your life. These uses include affordable access to information, staying connected, exposure to art and music, sharing schedules, etc.

Below, explore how technology positively affects you and how you will avoid overusing it to maintain overall healthy well-being.

Aspects of Life	How Technology Affects Me in a Positive Way	Things I Can Do to Avoid Technology Overuse
Example: *Physical Wellness*	*I track my daily exercise on my smartwatch.*	*I will not get obsessed with checking it and missing other aspects of my life.*
Physical Wellness		
Social Relationships		
Educational or Work Performance		
Emotional Well-Being		
Recreational Wellness		
Spiritual Health		
Other		

Destructive Effects of Technology

You need to learn to balance your use of technology with other areas of your life to maintain a balanced life and overall well-being. Overuse of technology can affect many aspects of your life, including weight gain, sleep issues, carpal tunnel syndrome, lack of friendships, relationship problems, lack of exercise, limited hobbies, issues at work or school, etc.

Below, explore how technology is negatively affecting you and how you might reduce your use of technology for overall healthy well-being.

Aspects of Life	How It Negatively Affects Me	How to Reduce Technology Use
Example: Physical Wellness	*I am not sleeping enough at night because I follow information rabbit holes.*	*I will stop using technology an hour before going to bed.*
Physical Wellness		
Social Relationships		
Educational or Work Performance		
Emotional Well-Being		
Recreational Wellness		
Spiritual Health		
Other		

Safe Driving

Technology is a wonderful tool when used properly, but it has its downsides. Many people are so addicted to technology that they text, email, search the internet, and talk on the phone while driving, putting themselves and others at risk.

Below, explore how you use technology when driving. Be honest.

How I Use Technology When Driving	How It Has or Can be Destructive	How I Can Be Safer
Example: I answer my cell phone if it rings.	I have not had a problem yet, but I know I am not as attentive to my driving as I should be.	Wait until I am at my destination. Then, call back.

Tips for not getting into an accident, hurting yourself, or others.

- Do not send or respond to text messages or phone calls while driving or at a red light because it puts you and others at risk and may be against the law.
- Turn off your phone and put it away.
- Use technology only when your car is parked in a safe place.
- Always stay focused on the road when you are driving.
- Concentrate 100% on the task at hand – driving.
- Speak up if you are in a car with someone texting or talking on the phone when driving.
- Turn off notifications and place your phone out of reach when you are in your vehicle.

Two Types of Interaction

Digital technology and social media make it easier for people to stay in touch, but they can also distract from in-person connections. Both types of interaction can contribute to social and emotional well-being.

Below, in the left-hand column, identify the benefits of communicating face-to-face (go out with friends and socialize, share ideas, spend face-to-face time, etc.).

Then, in the right-hand column, identify the benefits of communicating online (receiving support from multiple people, anonymity, feeling less isolated, etc.).

Face-to-Face Communication Benefits	**Online Communication Benefits**
_____	_____
_____	_____
_____	_____
_____	_____
_____	_____

Which form of communication do you use most? _____

_____

Why do you use that form the most? _____

_____

Why don't you use other forms of communication as much?_____

_____

Do you believe you have a healthy balance of online and face-to-face communications?_____

Explain why or why not? _____

_____

_____

_____

Technology Autopilot

You may not realize it, but you might be on autopilot regarding your technology use. Do you check your texts first thing in the morning? Do you compulsively check your emails? Do you mindlessly scroll online? Do you panic when the phone or computer isn't working right? Using technology this way can be anxiety-producing! Mindfulness practice, noticing your in-the-moment experience, can help you move from autopilot into awareness and choice.

Below, identify times you are on autopilot and grab for technology.

Times that I Am on Autopilot	What I Miss Out On	How I Can Be More Mindful
Example: The first thing I do in the morning is to grab my phone.	*I miss quality time with my family before everyone goes their way.*	*I could take my time to connect with my family before checking my phone.*

The Dark Side of Technology

Technology has a dark side, including cyberbullying, sexual exploitation, cybercrime, hacked personal information, credit card information, viruses, and physical issues *(vision problems, hearing loss, and neck strain).* Being overly plugged in can cause psychological issues such as distraction, narcissistic behavior, the expectation of instant gratification, low self-esteem, and even depression.

People who are <u>heavily</u> invested in technology are exposed to many risks. Below, identify how you have been a victim of the dark side of technology.

Dark Side of Technology	How I (or Someone I Know) Was Affected	How People Can Protect Themselves
Cyberbullying		
Sexual Exploitation		
Personal Information Hacked		
Credit Card Information Stolen		
Computer Viruses		
Physical Issues		
Psychological Issues		

Every aspect of human technology has a dark side, including the bow and arrow.
~ Margaret Atwood

Create Boundaries for Yourself

Below are some ways you can create boundaries between you and technology.

- Do not let your whole life be absorbed and surrounded by technology rather than people.
- Keep digital devices in a designated spot.
- Limit and monitor your technology usage.
- Set times when you will use technology and times when you will not.
- Set limits for certain apps and sites that can keep you from scrolling the day away.
- Take a day of rest when you will not use technology.

Below, describe the types of technology you use, how much you use it, and how you could use it less often.

Type of Technology	How Much I Use This Technology	How I Could Use This Technology Less	How I Could Make Use of the Time When I Don't Use It
Email			
Games			
Internet			
Smartphone			
Camera			
Other			

Recharging

With the plethora of technology you can access, it is essential to take some quiet time daily to relax, reflect, and even boost creativity. People who grab their phone or search social media sites constantly miss out on valuable opportunities to recharge their physical, emotional, and mental batteries. How can you set aside some time each day to disconnect and recharge?

In the circles below, identify some of the activities you can engage in to recharge (i.e., yoga, meditation, walking, etc.):

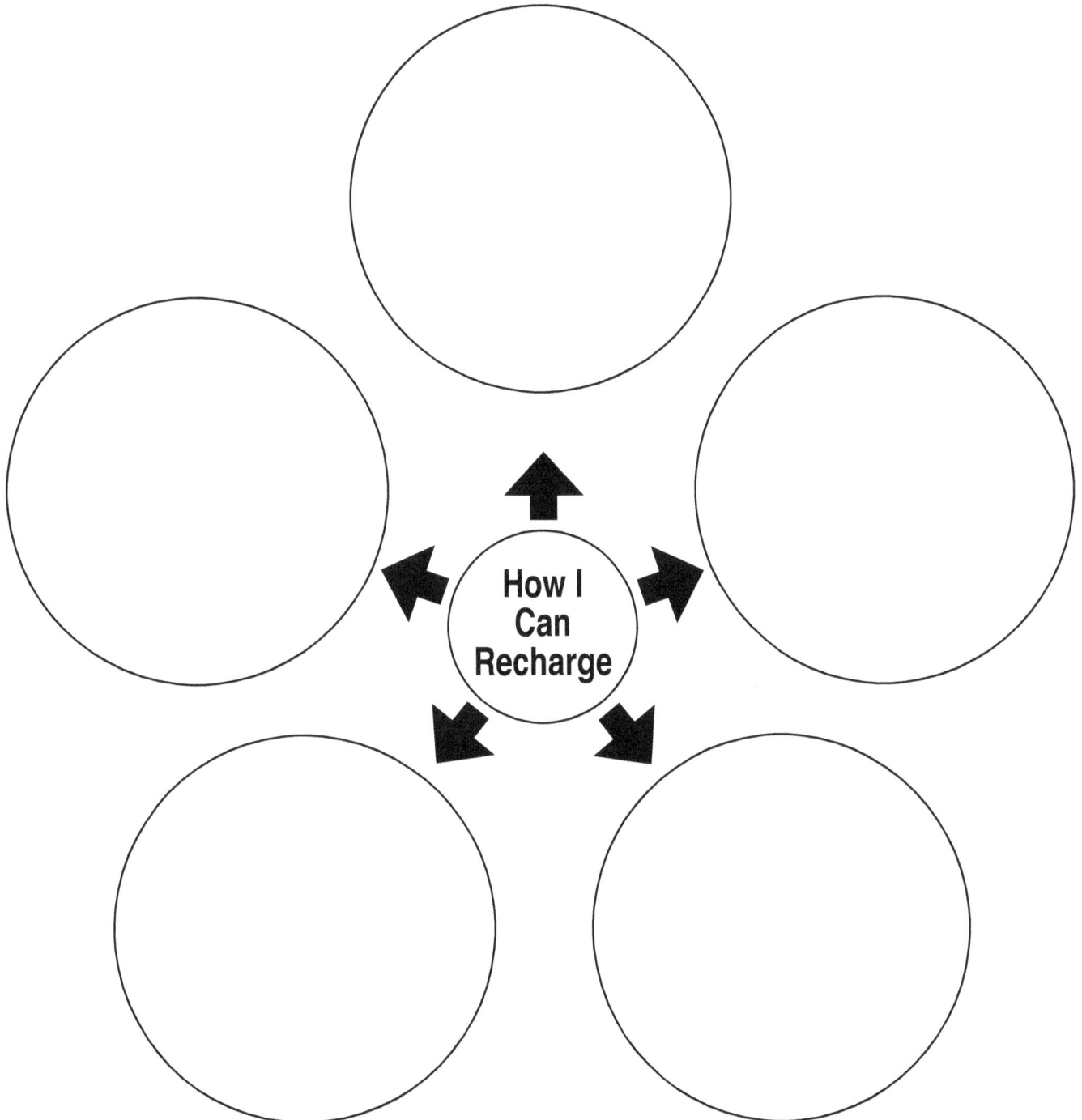

How I Can Recharge

Make Adjustments to Your Devices and Yourself

It is vital to explore ways to adjust your devices and yourself to use technology as efficiently and effectively as possible.

With each of the various ways below, journal about how you have made or will make the following adjustments.

Adjustments	Adjustments I Have Made	Adjustments I Will Make
Remove Distracting Apps		
Organize Your Apps		
Put the Screen on Black and White Which Is Much Less Distracting		
Remove Unimportant Notification Indicators		
Limit the Number of Times to Check Emails		
Limit the Number of Times to Check Texts		
When Busy, Call Later, or Do It Later		
Turn the Phone Off Unless You Are Anticipating an Emergency		
Other		

Single-Tasking

Most people addicted to technology must have their devices (smartphones, tablets, video games, etc.) available at all times. Because of this, they often multi-task and access technology while doing other things. Multitasking is often counterproductive to getting anything done well or done at all.

To improve focus, reduce the number of screens around you. Prioritize the one that helps you achieve a single task at a time.

Ways I Multi-Task	How I Am Distracted	How I Could Single-Task
Example: I eat breakfast while checking my email.	*I often don't even remember what I ate!*	*I could eat breakfast and then check emails when I get to where I'm going.*
Example: I search the internet while watching television.	*I miss half of what I am watching and forget half of what I am searching for.*	*Complete searching the internet, then watch television.*

Ways to Single-Task:
- Feel satisfied completing one task at a time.
- Focus on one task at a time.
- Keep only the devices you need with you.
- Notice when you are getting urges to multi-task and refocus on one task.
- Only use the technology devices you need to use.
- Put devices in *do not disturb* mode.
- Remove yourself from all tech distractions.

Unplugging

Living online is a regular, everyday occurrence for people who use a vast amount of technology. They don't just get online; they live online. What are some of the ways that you live online? Do you get up in the morning and check emails first thing, play video games long after bedtime, browse online for hours, etc.?

One of the best ways to unplug is to replace the technology habit with another habit. For example, you could replace a late-night shopping habit with a habit of meditating, replace texting with time spent talking face-to-face with friends or family, and time spent watching television can be replaced with reading a good book from the library.

Below, describe how you could replace some of your technology habits.

Technology I Use	Non-Technology Habits to Replace My Technology Habits
Example: Smartphone	*I often have several simultaneous text streams with multiple friends and lose track of who said what. I could organize group get-togethers more often.*
Smartphone	
Video Games	
Email	
TV	
Social Media Sites	
Internet Browsing	
Other	

New technology is not good or evil in and of itself.
It's all about how people choose to use it.
~ David Wong

Device-Free Zones and Times

Designate times of your day and spaces in your home to be device-free. Finding a central place to keep your phone can reduce the urge to check emails and notifications.

In the squares below, write the device-free zones in your home. Then next to the zone, note the times each zone will be device-free.

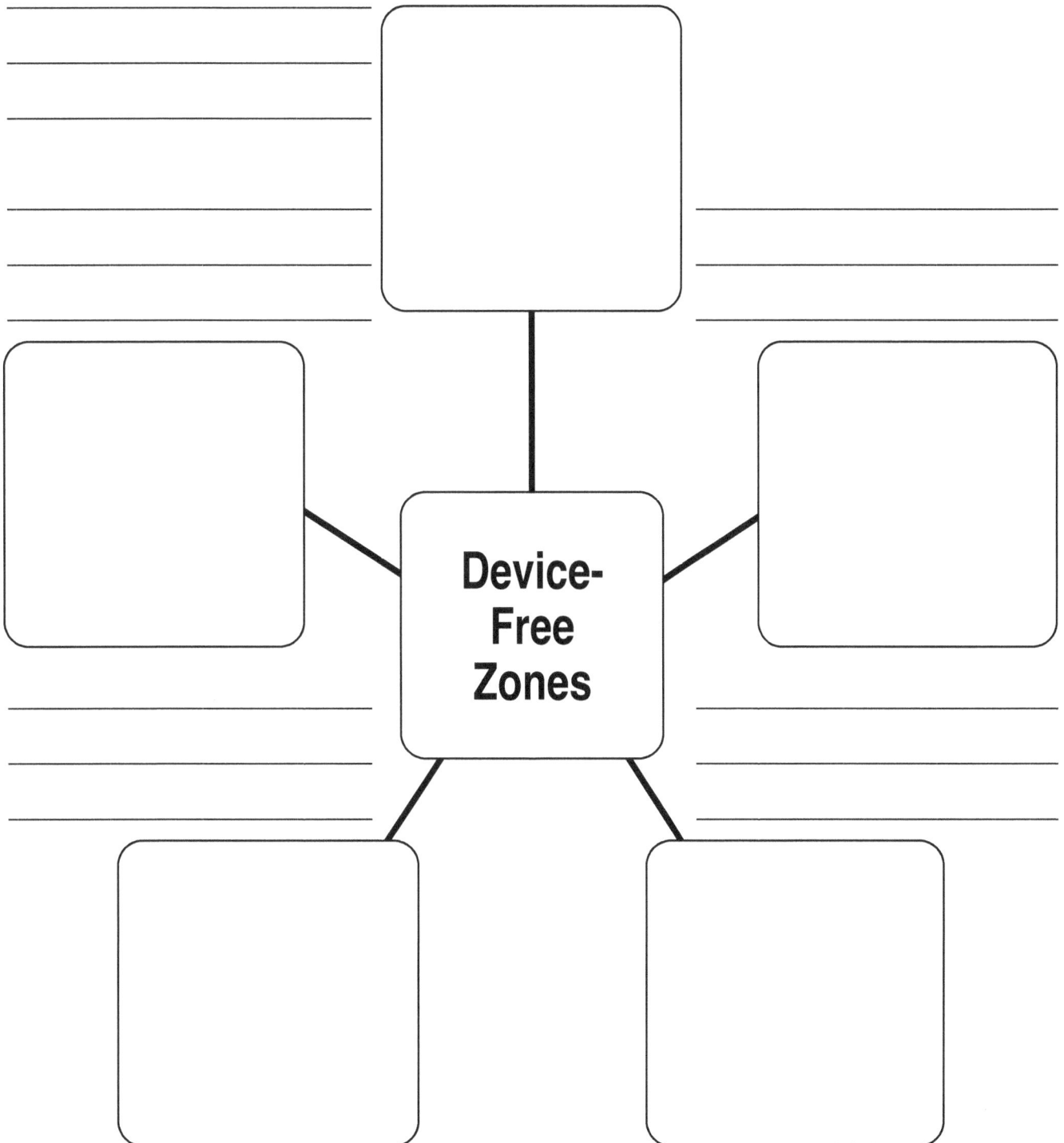

Wind Down for a Better Night's Sleep

Using technology to talk, search, or read keeps you stimulated. The use of technology late at night can significantly interfere with the quality of your sleep. You may be able to fall asleep, but the quality of your sleep can be a problem, leaving you tired or unsettled in the morning.

Creating space from technology late at night can help you feel more relaxed and help you sleep better.

Ways I will stop using my smartphone late at night.

Ways I will stop using my computer late at night.

Ways I will stop using my electronic reading device late at night.

Time Without Screens

It can be beneficial to consider various ways to spend time without screens. Think of some activities you could engage in rather than use technology. These activities might include walking or jogging, reading a print book, playing non-video games, visiting with friends, attending cultural or sporting events, spending time with family, playing sports, etc.

Below, write, draw, or doodle some of the non-technology-based activities you would like to engage in.

1.	2.
3.	4.
5.	6.

Rank the numbers in order of those you'd most like to do. _____ _____ _____ _____ _____ _____

Creating Connection

It is important to create connections in our age of technology and isolation. Technology can be a great way to do that, but it too often replaces in-person communication and socialization.

Identify the times you have felt socially isolated and how you can improve your social isolation.

Aspects of Social Isolation	My Situation	How I Can Improve My Social Isolation
Example: *I feel isolated socially.*	*I am shy. People have asked me to join them, and I have said NO. I am ready to try, but they no longer ask.*	*I think I will need the courage to invite some people I like to my home or out to a movie.*
I Feel Isolated Socially		
I Have Very Few Friends		
I Have Only a Few Friends Online		
I Primarily Communicate Via Technology		
I Spend a Lot of Time Staring at a Screen		
I Have Limited Social Skills		
Other		

Quotes About Digital Well-Being

On the lines that follow each of the quotes, describe how the quote speaks to you and your digital well-being.

Turn off your email; turn off your phone; disconnect from the internet; figure out a way to set limits so you can concentrate when you need to and disengage when you need to. Technology is a good servant but a bad master.
~ Gretchen Rubin

_____

_____

The human spirit must prevail over technology.
~ Albert Einstein

_____

_____

The great myth of our times is that technology is communication.
~ Libby Larsen

_____

_____

There are few times that I feel more at peace, more in tune, more Zen, if you will, than when I force myself to unplug.
~ Harlan Coben

_____

_____

Which quote especially speaks to you and your digital well-being? Why?

_____

_____

_____

_____

_____

_____

▼ Technology ▼

Unplugging

Name _____

Date _____

Technology Intensity Assessment
Introduction and Directions

People who are overusing technology have a difficult time unplugging. Often the greater the intensity of the addiction, the more difficult it is to unplug. Whether you like it or not, the best way to curb your overuse of technology is to force yourself to unplug. By unplugging, you can begin to reduce (NOT discontinue, but REDUCE) your use of technology and adopt a more low-tech lifestyle.

The *Technology Intensity Assessment* contains 20 statements that will help explore the intensity of your overuse of technology.

Read each of the statements and decide whether or not it describes you. If the statement describes you, circle the YES column next to that item. If the statement does not describe you, circle the NO column next to that item.

In the following example, the circled YES indicates that the statement describes the person completing this assessment:

Related to technology ...

I could not go a single day without technology . . . . (YES) . . . . NO

I check for phone messages even though my phone didn't ring . . . . (YES) . . . . NO

This is not a test. Since there are no right or wrong answers, do not spend too much time thinking about your answers. Be sure to respond to every statement. The purpose of this assessment is for YOU to learn more about YOU and your technology habits.

BE HONEST!

If you choose, no one else needs to see the results.

(Turn to the next page and begin.)

Technology Intensity Assessment

Name _____ Date _____

This will only be accurate if you respond honestly. No one else needs to see this if you choose.

Related to technology ...

I could not go a single day without technology ....YES...........NO

I check for phone messages even though my phone didn't ring ....YES...........NO

I check my phone every five minutes ....YES...........NO

I sleep with my phone by my bed...YES...........NO

I have a fear of missing out on things....................................YES...........NO

I feel the need to always be connected...................................YES...........NO

I am not satisfied unless I'm using technology.........................YES...........NO

I jump when I hear my cell phone ring ....YES...........NO

I take my cell phone to the bathroom just in case........................YES...........NO

Others close to me say I'm addicted to technology......................YES...........NO

I can't remember the last time I didn't have technology with me ....YES...........NO

I worry when no one is trying to contact me..............................YES...........NO

I use technology while I'm eating...YES...........NO

I am bored with non-technology activities or games.....................YES...........NO

I know that I am preoccupied with my devices ....YES...........NO

I often feel guilty about how I ignore people to use my devices ....YES...........NO

I lose the sense of time when using technology...........................YES...........NO

I get strong urges to use technology.....................................YES...........NO

I get a thrill from using my technology ....YES...........NO

I cannot cut down on my use of technology...............................YES...........NO

Technology Intensity "YES" TOTAL = _____

Go to the next page for scoring assessment results, profile interpretation, and individual description.

Technology Intensity Assessment

Scoring Descriptions and Profile Interpretation

The assessment you just completed is designed to measure your use or overuse of technology.

Count the number of YES answers you circled on the Technology Intensity Assessment. Put that total on the line marked TOTAL on the assessment at the bottom of the page. Then, transfer your total to the space below:

Technology Intensity "YES" TOTAL   =   _____

Assessment Profile Interpretation

By circling even one YES answer, you may be at risk of developing or having an addiction to technology. The more YES answers you circled, the greater your risk of experiencing a problem with your technology use.

Mark your total score on the continuum below.

The HIGHER your score on the *Technology Intensity Assessment*, the more of a technology issue you are experiencing.

0 = Low	10 = Moderate	20 = High

Were you honest when completing the assessment? _____ Is your score valid?

_____

_____

What is your reaction to your score?

_____

_____

Do you feel you need to do something about your score?

_____

_____

Reconnect with Myself

People who overuse their devices often have an addiction to technology. At times, it helps to disconnect from digital devices, which allows them to reconnect with themselves and be more intentional with how they spend their time. Reconnecting with yourself is not only about regaining time in your life. It's about ensuring that your time is spent with other things that are meaningful to you.

Write, draw, or doodle about how you will reconnect with yourself and find meaning beyond technology.

I am ...	The Purpose of my Life is to ...
My Favorite Non-Technology Thing to Do Is ...	My Dream is to ...

Life is without meaning. You bring the meaning to it.
The meaning of life is whatever you ascribe it to be.
Being alive is the meaning.
~ Joseph Campbell

Benefits of Unplugging

Unplugging is at the heart of overcoming your need to use your devices constantly. There are proven benefits to unplugging from various forms of technology. It can be challenging to unplug for people who overuse technology.

For each sentence starter, describe how your life might be better if you unplug.

My overall quality of life may improve because ...

_____

_____

My eating habits may improve because ...

_____

_____

My sleeping habits may improve because ...

_____

_____

My energy may increase because ...

_____

_____

My work performance may improve because ...

_____

_____

My family relationships may improve because ...

_____

_____

My friendships may improve because ...

_____

_____

Mindful Eating

It may seem like a simple thing to do, but people who overuse technology must put their devices (phones, televisions, social media apps, computers, video games, etc.) away while sharing a meal with family and friends. This allows more face-to-face conversation time. People who excessively use technology don't tend to eat very mindfully. Some of these non-mindful behaviors are listed below.

On the line under each sentence listed below, place an X on the continuum of how much you relate to the statement. On the dotted line below each one, write why you rated yourself that way. **BE HONEST!**

I gobble meals quickly so I can get back to my technology.

0 (Not Like Me)   5 (Somewhat Like Me)   10 (Much Like Me)

I use my devices while I eat my meal or have a snack.

0 (Not Like Me)   5 (Somewhat Like Me)   10 (Much Like Me)

I will not sit down at a meal without my technology close by.

0 (Not Like Me)   5 (Somewhat Like Me)   10 (Much Like Me)

I don't appreciate my food because I want to use my technology.

0 (Not Like Me)   5 (Somewhat Like Me)   10 (Much Like Me)

I refuse to put technology away while I am eating my meals.

0 (Not Like Me)   5 (Somewhat Like Me)   10 (Much Like Me)

I do not notice anything but technology when I am eating or snacking.

0 (Not Like Me)   5 (Somewhat Like Me)   10 (Much Like Me)

HIGHER SCORES (Much Like Me) on many of the statements indicate that you probably have a technology addiction.

MEDIUM SCORES (Somewhat Like Me) other than getting a zero indicate a possible technology addiction problem.

LOWER SCORES (Not Like Me) suggest that you are not experiencing many signs of a technology problem.

Relaxation

People who overuse technology can consciously or unconsciously neglect themselves. They are habitually super busy, on the go, plugged in, talking, binge-watching TV programs and movies, or using other forms of technology.

All people, especially people addicted to technology, need to do things to relax other than passively using technology. Whether going to a movie theater, listening to music, dancing, doing yoga, meditating, playing sports, getting a massage, or taking a run or walk, you need to relax and take care of yourself.

Identify the activities you can use to unplug from technology, unwind, and relax.

Relaxing Activities	How They Will Help Me Relax	When I Will Do Them
Example: Gardening	It helps me relax by doing something physical and allows me to see something grow.	Right after dinner.

Place a check by your activities in the first column that can provide the following positive effects of relaxation.
- Reduced risk of stress-related illnesses.
- The power to better resist future stressors.
- A more positive outlook on life and your experiences.
- The ability to think more clearly and make better decisions.
- A healthier body, slower breathing rate, relaxed muscles, and reduced blood pressure.

What Am I Missing?

If you have been overusing technology, it is time to unplug!

Using the form below, list how overuse impacts your life, what you miss out on while overusing technology, or how overuse prevents you from being productive and making meaningful in-person connections.

Overuse of Technology	What Am I Missing?	In-Person Connections I Could Make (USE NAME CODES)
Example: Watching hours and hours of television.	In-person friends to socialize with and have fun with. Face-to-face conversations.	In-person friends to socialize with and have fun with. Face-to-face conversations. I could ask MHS and GTO if they would like to get a bite to eat and go bowling or to the movies.

If you don't get on the field and play, then you will be missing out.
~ Michael Schenker

What does this quote mean to you and your overuse of technology? _____

_____

_____

_____

When I Unplug Some of the Time

What would you like to do when you unplug? What could you do with the available time to enjoy other things? When you do unplug, you will need low-tech activities to fill your time.

Identify the activities you would like to try when unplugging for some of the time. Identify the activities you would like to participate in from the first column to replace some of the time and energy you spend with your use of technology.

Types of Activities	Things I Could Do and Enjoy	Technology I Would Replace
Example: Creativity	*Oil painting on a canvas.*	*Searching social media sites right after dinner.*
Creativity		
Social		
Nature		
Animal		
Mechanical		
Family		
Sports		
Business		
Cooking/Baking		
Other		
Other		

Time to Reconnect

It may be time to decrease your technology time, unplug, and spend quality time connecting in person with family and friends as you renew yourself. Often our lives get so busy that we can spend months without connecting face-to-face with close friends or family.

Schedule a time to get together, and use that time to catch up on life. Before you leave, try to schedule another time to meet. Continue doing that until it becomes a habit. Commit to staying in touch with others more often. When doing this, put away your cell phone and other types of technology. In the following squares, identify the people you want to spend time with and why.

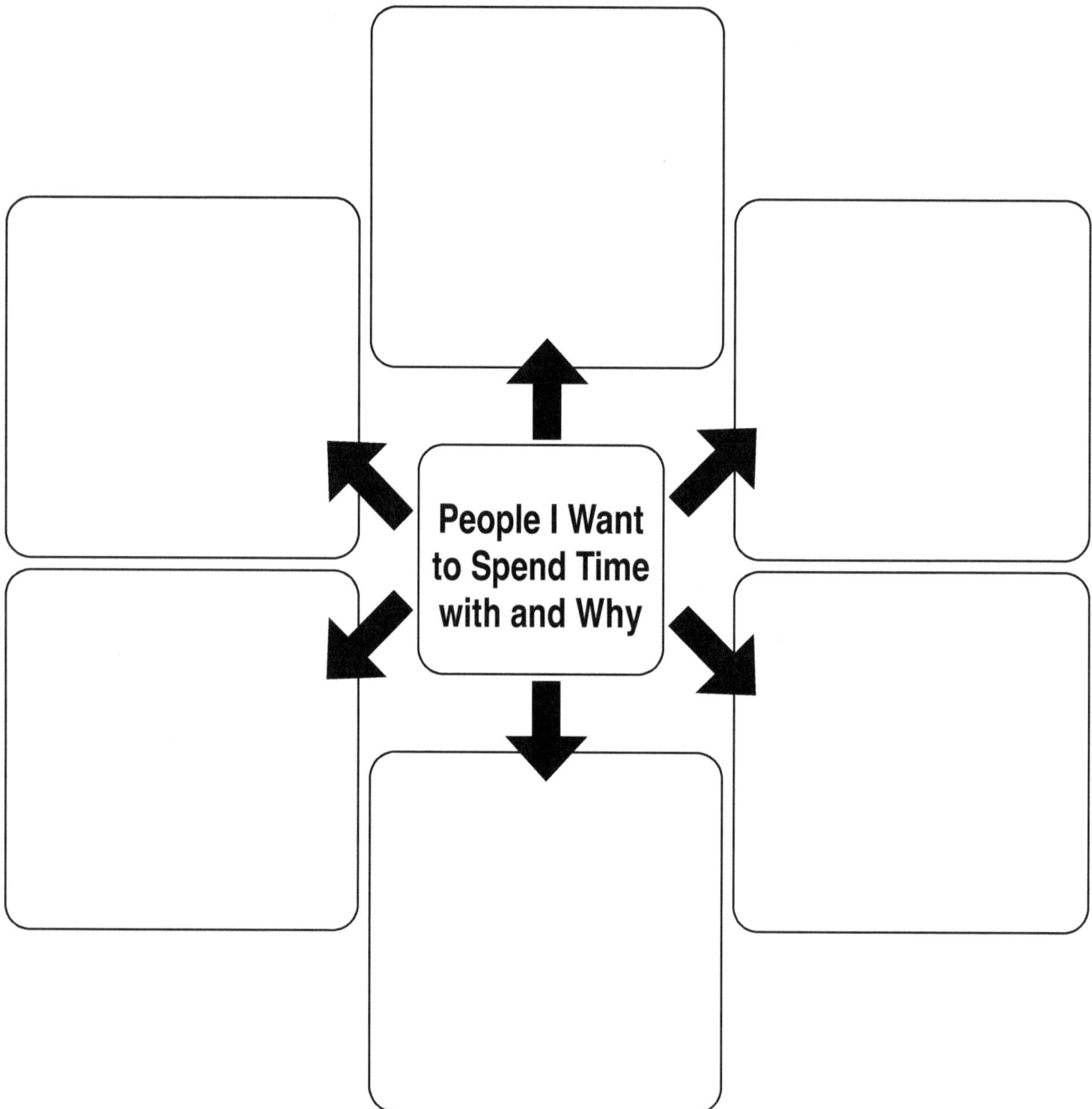

People I Want to Spend Time with and Why

Unplugging at Night

Excessive technology use, especially an hour or two before bedtime, can disturb your natural sleep cycle and make you tired the next day. Adults need seven to nine hours of sleep to stay healthy, function well, and recharge. When you choose a healthy sleep routine, you will feel better, be more productive the next day, be less stressed, and enjoy your life more.

Here are some tips for unplugging at night. Describe how you will use those that seem like they will work for you. You may choose not to use each one.

Set a strict technology-free bedtime when you will not watch TV, look at a computer screen, check emails, or use your phone. Try this about two hours before you go to bed so you will have time to wind down.

_____

_____

_____

To avoid disturbing your sleep, set your phone on silent or sleep mode except for your morning alarm.

_____

_____

_____

Do not check emails while in bed. Your emails can wait until morning.

_____

_____

_____

Don't take your phone into your bedroom.

_____

_____

_____

Get rid of the TV in your room. This can be a tough one.

_____

_____

_____

Meditation in the Morning

Many people wake up and automatically reach for their cell phones. When you do this, you begin each morning in a stressful manner rather than waking up, stretching, and feeling rejuvenated, renewed, and relaxed. Try starting your day with meditation. Even if you don't have much time, a few minutes of quiet reflection can start you off on the right track.

Instead of reaching for your phone as soon as you wake up, try this progressive relaxation:

- Continue to lie in bed and close your eyes.

- Take four or five slow, extended breaths.

- Focus your attention on your feet and notice how they feel. Feel the weight of the backs of your heels flat against the mattress. Tense your feet, then as consciously as possible, begin to relax them.

- Do this with the rest of your body. Slowly work your way up your body like you tensed and relaxed your feet. Do the same for your calves, thighs, hips, stomach, and chest.

- Now do the same for your hands (make them into fists), arms, shoulders, neck, and face.

- Always do one part of your body before moving to the next (one leg at a time, one arm at a time, etc.).

- Move from the bottom and work your way up your body. You can relax individual parts of your face, including your eyes, forehead, temples, lips, and cheeks.

- Finish by taking one last breath, and then open your eyes.

Try this for a few mornings, and then write about what you noticed.

_____

_____

_____

_____

_____

_____

_____

_____

Progressive relaxation is a muscle skill. Just as you would practice the piano or shooting baskets, becoming skilled at meditation takes time and repetition.

Write a Letter or Thank You Note

Social media is not the only way to connect with people. Yes, you can still write letters or thank-you notes the old-school way (write, put it in an envelope, address it, put on a stamp, and mail it!) and connect with your friends and family. How long has it been since you've written a letter or a thank-you note to a friend instead of a quick text or email?

In each of the blocks below, identify a person with whom you want to connect, reconnect, or thank. Describe what you would say in a hand-written letter or thank-you note.

Person's Name Code _____

What I Would Say:

Person's Name Code _____

What I Would Say:

Person's Name Code _____

What I Would Say:

Now write your letters and send them. Aren't you curious if you will hear back from them, and how?

Leave Work at Work

Leave it at work when you have finished your day. People addicted to technology often work throughout the evening, checking work emails from home. This encourages the overuse of technology. One of the ways you can leave work at work is to put an auto-reply message that says, "Thank you for your email. I'm away from my desk, and I look forward to responding to your message upon my return." Resist the temptation to check emails and updates after work. Do not check work voicemails from home. Leave them until the next day. In this way, you're helping yourself unplug from technology and the job.

In the hexagons below, identify some ways you will leave your work at work.

Ways to Leave Work at Work

Become More Active

To unplug from technology you will benefit from becoming more active. What are some of the ways you can become more active? *(Examples: exercise, Zumba, martial arts, yoga, walking, jogging, running, working out in a gym, weight training, gardening, walking a dog, etc.)*

When you unplug and exercise your heart rate increases, your body moves, and endorphins flow to your brain. You benefit your health and will likely be able to take your mind off other stressors in your life and keep yourself from plugging in constantly!

Below, write about, draw, or doodle four ways you will become more active.

1.	2.
3.	4.

Physical activity—even if you don't lose an ounce, you'll live longer, feel healthier
and be less likely to get cancer, heart disease, stroke, and arthritis.
It's the closest thing we have to a wonder drug.
~ Tom Frieden

Do Something for Others

A great way to unplug is to do things for others. Rather than talking on the phone or surfing the internet, do something for someone else. Put your technology away and allow yourself some time to be there for someone in need. This can be as simple as helping someone with an errand.

Below, identify some of the people and organizations you could help in some way.

People I Can Help USE NAME CODES	What I Can Do	How This Can Help Them and Me
Example: Homeless people	*Volunteer at the local homeless shelter. I could help out at dinner time.*	*I could make a difference in their lives and surf the net less often.*

Some additional ways to be helpful:

- Assist senior neighbors by bringing their newspapers to the door.
- Help someone do yard work or cut their lawn.
- Listen to a friend in need.
- Pick up groceries for someone and help put them away.
- Read to older people in a rehab facility.
- Tutor someone who is struggling.
- Volunteer at a local food bank.
- Walk animals at the local shelter.

I Might Miss Out!

A constant stream of notifications, alerts, updates, and social media streams bombard people with continuous information. Many people who overuse technology are afraid of missing something happening with their friends, family, or in the news. It is important to realize that if it's something vital, you will find out about it without constantly checking your devices.

Think about those things that you are afraid of missing. How can you resolve the fact that you can check your devices every once in a while rather than constantly?

Technology	How I am Afraid of Missing Out	What If I Wait until my Technology Time
Example: Social Media	*I might not see a friend request.*	*I will see it later in the day...no problem!*
Social Media		
Television		
Smartphone		
Internet		
Video Games		
Other		

Delayed gratification is a sweet lesson whose
teacher knows the best is not right now, it is yet to be.
~ Maximillian Degenerez

Do More Things Offline

When you overuse technology, you are living your life electronically and virtually. It is important to unplug and allow yourself to have fun, enjoy yourself and others, think about life, cry at a sad movie, meditate, read a book offline, go on a date, and be active.

Below, write about some things you can do offline to unplug and slow down your technology addiction.

Things I Could Do Offline	How It Will Help Me Reduce My Technology Addiction
Example: Read a book from the library.	*I will not be using electronic media.*

There'll come a writing phase where you have to defend the time,
unplug the phone and put in the hours to get it done.
~ James Taylor

Quotes about Unplugging from Technology

On the lines that follow each of the quotes, describe how the quote speaks to you and how it applies to your life.

Cyberspace can't compensate for real space.
We benefit from chatting to people face to face.
~ Jonathan Sacks

_____

_____

When it comes to social media, there are just times I turn off the world, you know.
There are just sometimes you must give yourself space to be quiet,
which means you've got to set those phones down.
~ Michelle Obama

_____

_____

You practice mindfulness, on the one hand, to be calm and peaceful.
On the other hand, as you practice mindfulness and live a life of peace,
you inspire hope for a future of peace.
~ Thich Nhat Hanh

_____

_____

Cell phones, e-mail, and all the other cool and slick gadgets can cause
massive losses in our creative output and overall productivity.
~ Robin S. Sharma

_____

_____

Which quote especially speaks to you about unplugging from technology? Why?

_____

_____

_____

_____

Technology

Finding Balance

Name _____

Date _____

Technology Assessment
Introduction and Directions

In today's world, technology is available 24/7. It is easier than ever to overuse technology and just as easy to become addicted to it. Exploring and being aware of the various types of technology is important.

The *Technology Assessment* contains 25 statements related to the five major types of technology to which people are addicted. It will help you gauge how much you use each type of technology.

Read each of the statements and decide whether it describes you. If the statement describes you, circle the number in the YES column next to that item. If the statement does not describe you, circle the number in the NO column next to that item. Ignore the number. Just circle the YES or NO.

In the following example, the circled 2 indicates that the person completing this assessment believes that the statement describes them:

	YES	NO
When it comes to watching television ...		
I spend large amounts of time watching TV.	(2)	1
I often find myself watching more than I intended	(2)	1

This is not a test. Since there are no right or wrong answers, do not spend too much time thinking about your answers. Be sure to respond to every statement. The purpose of this assessment is for YOU to learn more about YOU and your technology habits.

BE HONEST!

If you choose, no one else needs to see the results.

(Turn to the next page and begin.)

Technology Assessment (Page 1)

Name _____ Date _____

This will only be accurate if you respond honestly. No one else needs to see this if you choose.

	YES	NO

When it comes to watching television ...

I spend large amounts of time watching TV 2 1

I often find myself watching more than I intended 2 1

I would rather watch TV than do most other things 2 1

I use television as a stimulant 2 1

I am mindlessly flipping through the stations 2 1

Television TOTAL = _____

	YES	NO

In searching the internet ...

I can search for different interesting items for hours and hours 2 1

I attempt to hide the amount of time I spend online 2 1

I become angry if people try to talk to me when I am online 2 1

I have trouble limiting the amount of time I spend online 2 1

Other aspects of my life suffer because of my time online 2 1

Internet TOTAL = _____

	YES	NO

When using social media ...

I have more friends on social media than I have in real life 2 1

I rely too much on social media to cope with my problems 2 1

I join all new social media sites as they become available 2 1

I stay up ridiculously late using social media 2 1

I check my social media sites no matter where I am 2 1

Social Media TOTAL = _____

(Continued on the next page.)

Technology Assessment (Page 2)

Name _____ Date _____

This will only be accurate if you respond honestly. No one else needs to see this if you choose.

	YES	NO

When it comes to gaming ...

I often can't think about anything other than gaming 2 1

I only have online friends that I game with 2 1

I have jeopardized many of my relationships because of gaming 2 1

I neglect all other activities when I am gaming 2 1

I have noticed a reduction in my work and various obligations 2 1

Gaming TOTAL = _____

	YES	NO

When it comes to my smartphone ...

I use it when I'm bored... 2 1

I often don't care who I call, I just want to use my phone................ 2 1

I depend on my phone too much 2 1

I automatically use it when I feel lonely 2 1

I become upset when I try to connect with someone who can't 2 1

Smartphone TOTAL = _____

Go to the next page for scoring assessment results, profile interpretation, and individual description.

Technology Assessment

Scoring Descriptions and Profile Interpretation

The assessment you just completed is designed to measure the types of technology you tend to overuse or are dependent on.

In each of the sections on the previous pages, count the scores you circled. Put that number on the line marked TOTAL at the end of each section. Transfer your total to the space below and place an X on the line representing your score:

Television = _____ **(The time you spend watching tv.)**

_____
5 = Low   8 = Moderate   10 = High

Internet = _____ **(The time you spend searching the internet.)**

_____
5 = Low   8 = Moderate   10 = High

Social Media = _____ **(The time you spend accessing and interacting on social media sites.)**

_____
5 = Low   8 = Moderate   10 = High

Gaming = _____ **(The time you spend playing video games.)**

_____
5 = Low   8 = Moderate   10 = High

Smartphone = _____ **(The time you spend interacting with your smartphone.)**

_____
5 = Low   8 = Moderate   10 = High

Assessment Profile Interpretation

Even one circled item on a scale can suggest you are overusing your technology devices. The HIGHER your score in each area, the greater the effect overuse of technology has on your life.

How about Offline Highs?

You probably find yourself feeling high when you are engaging with technology online. People who overuse online technology find that it allows them to do or talk about things that are not always happening or available offline. It is important to think about various ways you can experience healthy offline highs to compensate for a reduction in the use of technology. How can you experience healthy, offline highs?

Type of Technology	The High I Receive from It	How I Can Have a Healthy, Offline High
Example: Cell Phone	*I don't have a lot of friends, so I call people I game with to talk, and then we usually end up playing.*	*I could join the reading club at the local library and interact face-to-face with other people who enjoy the same books.*
Cell Phone		
Social Media		
Gaming		
Sports on Television		
Computer		
Tablet		
Other		

I'm Tired

Too much time plugged in can leave you feeling overwhelmed, stressed, exhausted, and overworked. Stepping away from technology screens can seem impossible to do.

Below, explore how your overuse of technology makes you feel and how you can step away from it.

For example, you may start getting eye strain from gaming too much, so you may tell the other gamers you are taking a break and start walking instead.

Ways I Am Available to Everyone with Technology	How I Sometimes Feel from Technology Overuse	How I Can Step Away from Technology
Example: I try to be available whenever anyone wants me to be, no matter what.	*My eyes have been hurting, and I need to get to the eye doctor.*	*I need to say NO when I don't want to game. I need to stop being available and pleasing everyone.*

It has become appallingly obvious that our technology has exceeded our humanity.
~ Albert Einstein

What do you think Albert Einstein would say about today's technology?

_____

_____

_____

Being Out of Balance

Being out of balance can have devastating costs, personally and professionally. What is the cost of your overuse of technology and inability to find a life balance concerning your health, work, relationships, etc.?

Life Areas Affected by Technology Overuse	How Technology Overuse Affects My Life
Example: Work	*I'm continually drawn to check social media, and I fall behind on my work.*
Pain From Sitting Too Much	
Deficits in Social Skills	
Eating Habits	
Family	
Finances	
Health	
Need for Instant Gratification	
Relationships	
Sadness or Frustration	
Sense of Isolation	
Sleep	
Work	
Other	

Am I Disconnected?

Many people who overuse technology find that unless they find more innovative ways to use it, they are in danger of becoming disconnected from themselves, others, and the world in general. Some athletic people watch sports on television rather than play football with friends.

Below, identify the ways you disconnect because of technology and ways you can connect without technology. It could be in your relationships, at work, at home, in leisure, etc.

Example:

***Ways I disconnect** – I scroll online for hours!*   ***Ways to connect** – Meet a friend for dinner.*

Ways I Disconnect	**Ways to Connect**
⇩	⇩
⇩	⇩
⇩	⇩
⇩	⇩
⇩	⇩

Balancing Relationships

If you overuse technology, many of your relationships likely consist of people online. Rather than developing in-person relationships, most of your communication is probably typed rather than spoken. While technology offers opportunities to connect with more people from more places, keeping a balance between face-to-face and digital connections is important. Develop your communication skills or you may lose them.

Many skills are associated with good communication. Check the boxes in front of the skills you currently possess. Then, put a check after each of the skills you want to develop and work on.

Messaging Skills
When I am communicating with another person ...
- ☐ I use "I Statements" when expressing my emotions. . . . . ☐
- ☐ I make sure that others understand what I say. . . . . ☐
- ☐ I express myself without prejudice or stereotypes. . . . . ☐
- ☐ I give direct messages. . . . . ☐
- ☐ I self-disclose appropriate information about myself. . . . . ☐

Body Language Skills
When I am communicating with another person ...
- ☐ I maintain eye contact with them. . . . . ☐
- ☐ I can read their body language. . . . . ☐
- ☐ I keep my body posture open and relaxed. . . . . ☐
- ☐ I maintain effective boundaries and respect the boundaries of others. . . . . ☐
- ☐ I am aware of when body language messages change. . . . . ☐

Attention Skills
When I am communicating with another person ...
- ☐ I listen to the other person and do not allow myself to become distracted. . . . . ☐
- ☐ I listen for the meaning and intent of the words said. . . . . ☐
- ☐ I listen as carefully as possible. . . . . ☐
- ☐ I try not to read the other person's mind or anticipate what they will say. . . . . ☐
- ☐ I do not interrupt the person speaking. . . . . ☐

Response Skills
When I am communicating with another person ...
- ☐ I stay focused and respond appropriately. . . . . ☐
- ☐ I do not think about my response while the person is talking. . . . . ☐
- ☐ I am non-judgmental about what the person says. . . . . ☐
- ☐ I am not easily distracted in the middle of a conversation. . . . . ☐
- ☐ I respond in an empathetic and caring manner. . . . . ☐

Which communication skills do you need to work on the most? _____

Work-Life Balance

Technology has made work-life balance almost impossible because of the connection to the internet, emails, and texting outside of regular work hours. The various ways to keep connected to work-related projects make it more challenging to maintain a work-life balance.

Below, identify some ways you can balance work and life by restricting excessive use of technology.

Ways My Work-Life Balance is Off Due to Technology	How I Feel About It	What I Do as a Result	What I Can Do
Example: I can be accessed by my supervisors at any time!	I need to keep checking my emails and cannot relax.	I stay online until I go to bed.	Explain to my supervisors I will only check my email during my scheduled hours.

I'm a workaholic. Before long I'm traveling on my nervous energy alone.
This is incredibly exhausting.
~ Eva Gabor

Loneliness

Many people reach for technology (video games, streaming services, phones, social media sites, etc.) to overcome their loneliness.

Complete the assessment that follows to help you explore your level of loneliness. This scale contains 25 statements. Read each statement and decide how closely the statement describes you. Each statement will either be LIKE ME or NOT LIKE ME. Circle the number of your response to the right of each statement.

	LIKE ME	NOT LIKE ME
In my offline life …		
I am completely alone.	2	1
I am isolated socially.	2	1
I am left out and out of touch.	2	1
I am lonely.	2	1
I am no longer close to anyone offline	2	1
I am starved for company when I am offline.	2	1
I am unhappy because I do almost everything by myself.	2	1
I don't have any companionship when I am offline.	2	1
I don't know how to reach out and communicate with others.	2	1
I feel shut out and excluded by others	2	1
I find it very difficult to make friends.	2	1
I hate being so isolated.	2	1
I have no one to talk with when I am in trouble.	2	1
I isolate from others	2	1
I know that nobody really cares for me offline.	2	1
I lack social support.	2	1
I need face-to-face social interactions	2	1
I wait for people to invite me to do things, and they don't.	2	1
I wish I could connect with people offline	2	1
My interests are not shared by people in my life.	2	1
My offline social relationships are superficial	2	1
My social needs are not met offline.	2	1
No one really knows me well enough to do things offline	2	1
People are around me but not with me	2	1
There is no one offline with whom I am friends	2	1

Loneliness TOTAL = _____

Add the numbers you've circled. Put that total on the line marked Loneliness TOTAL above. Then put an X that designates your score on the line below.

This scale measures the extent of your loneliness in your life offline.

25 = Not Very Lonely	38 = Very Lonely	50 = Extremely Lonely

Won't You Be My Neighbor?

You can develop face-to-face relationships by being more neighborly.

Fred Rogers said, "All of us, at some time or other, need help. Whether we're giving or receiving help, each one of us has something valuable to bring to this world. That's one of the things that connects us as neighbors in our own way, each one of us is a giver and a receiver."

Not only will being neighborly help you develop social relationships, but it will also give you something to do other than focusing on technology and make you feel as good as the neighbor you befriended.

Identify four neighbors with whom you could be more neighborly and how you can connect with them.

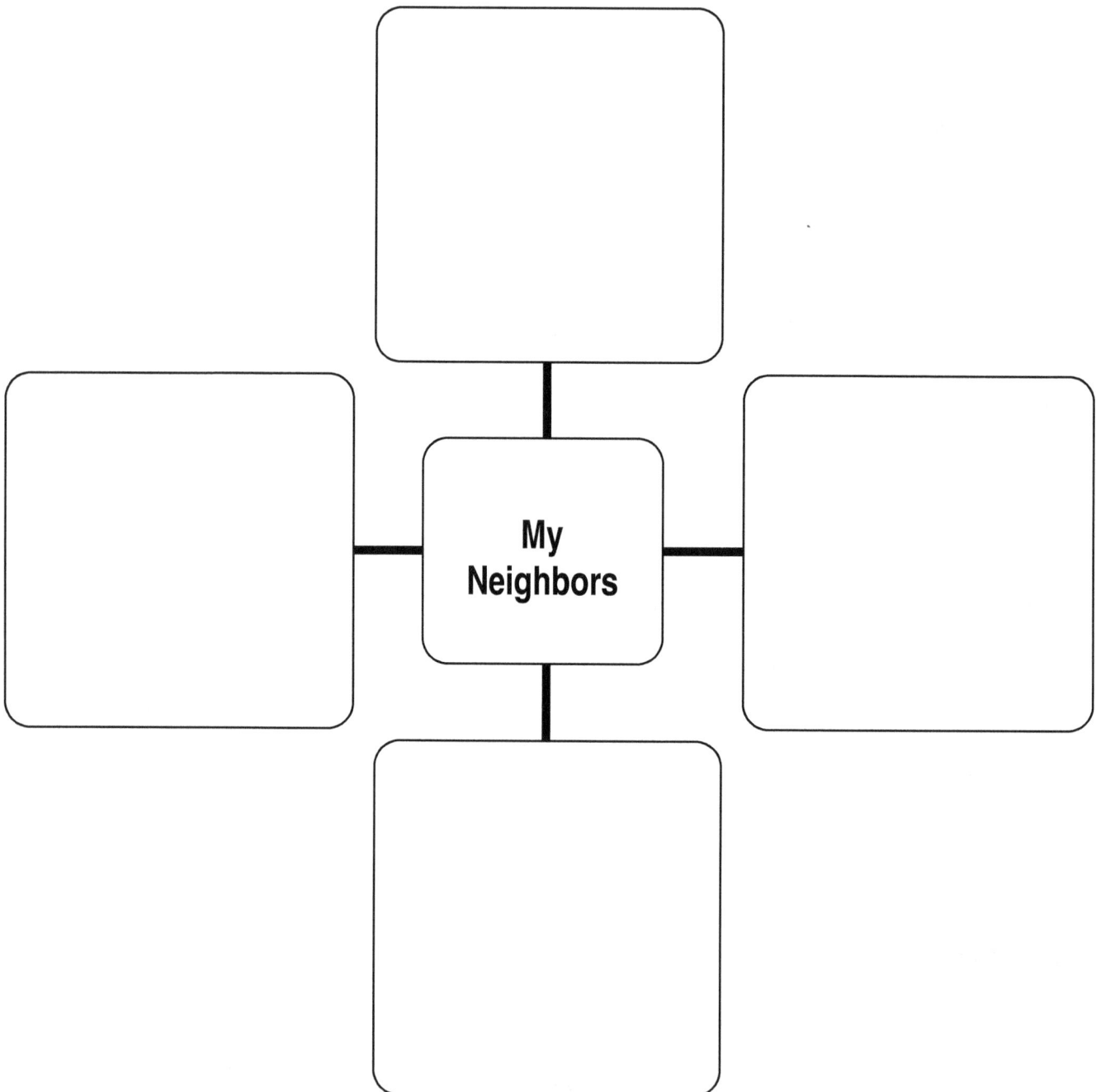

```
         ┌─────────────┐
         │             │
         │             │
         └──────┬──────┘
                │
┌──────────┐ ┌──┴───────┐ ┌──────────┐
│          │ │   My     │ │          │
│          ├─┤ Neighbors├─┤          │
│          │ │          │ │          │
└──────────┘ └──┬───────┘ └──────────┘
                │
         ┌──────┴──────┐
         │             │
         │             │
         └─────────────┘
```

Human Interactions

Face-to-face interactions allow people who overuse technology to laugh, experience empathy, chat, cry, share experiences, reminisce, and care! People miss many high-intensity interactions and feelings by only engaging in online relationships and using technology.

For each way these relationships can help you, identify some of the people with whom you interact (or can interact) to gain benefits.

Face-to-Face Interaction Benefits	Person I Can Interact with Face-to-Face and Why I Selected Them (USE NAME CODES)	How It Will Help Me
Example: Laugh	*MFH is a joyful neighbor of mine, always smiling and making me laugh.*	*I'll get to know her better and laugh more often.*
Laugh		
Experience Empathy		
Chat		
Cry		
Share Experiences		
Reminisce		
Other		

I remind myself that I'm always more satisfied by
human interaction than by a digital connection.
~ Maulik Pancholy

"I've Been Meaning To ..."

People who get so wrapped up in technology forget to do things they want or need to do. Consider your list of those things "I've been meaning to ..." *For example, you may have always wanted to learn ballroom dancing, join a cycling club, reach out to an old friend or family member, repaint your living room, go on a vacation with the family, or tutor children.*

For the sentence starter below, identify a list of things you've been meaning to do.

I've been meaning to ...

_____   _____

_____   _____

_____   _____

_____   _____

_____   _____

_____   _____

Put 2 stars by those that you __WILL__ do within the month!
Put 1 star by those that you __WILL__ do within two months!

Living Out of Balance

When you overuse technology, you will find that your body gets out of balance. The excessive use of technology devices causes physical problems.

Are you experiencing any physical problems stemming from the overuse of your devices? Describe them following the descriptions below.

Sedentary Lifestyle: The more time you spend with technology, the less time you have for physical fitness. Problems could include excessive weight gain or loss, musculoskeletal symptoms, heart problems, etc.

_____

_____

Vision: The prolonged use of devices could cause visual symptoms (e.g., discomfort, bloodshot eyes, eyestrain, blurred vision, migraine headache).

_____

_____

Injuries: Devices are often used while carrying out other tasks (i.e., walking, driving) and may cause the user to be more susceptible to accidents.

_____

_____

Social Development: More time spent on online engagement instead of face-to-face interaction can hinder social skill development or cause social withdrawal and loneliness.

_____

_____

Sleep Deprivation: The overuse of devices can cut into your sleep cycle and can cause you to be wired, sleepy, lethargic, and unable to rest.

_____

_____

Personal Concerns: Excessive use of technology has been associated with personal issues such as loneliness, little self-confidence, anxiety, sadness, low emotional stability, and low life satisfaction.

_____

_____

Out of Balance?

Balance is critical in life. People who overuse technology tend to begin to lose their life balance. They get so obsessed with technology that they don't want to interact any other way.

Look at the following quote and answer the questions that follow it.

For the self-conscious or insecure girl, technology can become a crippling addiction, an insatiable hunger not just for connection but the elusive promise of being liked by everyone.
~ Rachel Simmons

What does the quote mean to you?

_____

_____

_____

In what ways are you self-conscious and insecure?

_____

_____

_____

How has technology become an insatiable hunger?

_____

_____

_____

How have you used technology to connect with others? Is it enough, or do you need more?

_____

_____

_____

Do you think technology helps you be liked or have good, long-lasting friends?

_____

_____

_____

Go Outside

People who overuse technology devices spend most of their time indoors. Whether watching television, surfing the internet, searching social media sites, gaming, emailing, etc., most of the time technology use is indoors. It is crucial to participate in activities outside the house, to meet new people, do new things, be outside, exercise, and interact offline.

It may be time to move out of your comfort zone and seek out activities that interest you outside of technology. In the spaces that follow, write about, draw, or doodle four things you want to start doing outside.

Outside, I will …	Outside, I will …
Outside, I will …	**Outside, I will …**

Rediscover Technology Alternatives

What are some of the ways you could swap a high-tech activity for a low-tech activity?

For example, you could close your eyes and meditate rather than grab your phone. Another example would be to walk your dog in the park rather than surfing the internet.

What are some ways you could swap high-tech activities for low-tech ones?

High-Tech Activities	Low-Tech Activities
Example: Playing video games at night.	*Play board games with my children.*

Break Up with the Level of Your Technology

Detoxing totally from technology can be difficult and is probably not necessary. A reasonable digital detox is an excellent strategy for escaping technology overuse and for finding a tech-life balance. You will need to start slowly and reduce either the time spent or the people you are involved with; those people you feel suck you into more and more technology.

Provide yourself with small, manageable mini-goals to begin reducing your technology habit. Write about three of your mini-goals for TV, computer or tablet, and smartphone use below:

Detoxing from Technology

Televisions	Computers	Phones

Quotes about Balancing Life and Technology

On the lines that follow each of the quotes, describe how the quote speaks to you and how it applies to your life.

The point isn't to live without any regrets.
The point is to not hate ourselves for having them.
~ Kathryn Schulz

_____

_____

Human interaction is not a simple thing.
~ Julie Payette

_____

_____

Technological progress has merely provided us with more
efficient means for going backwards.
~ Aldous Huxley

_____

_____

Which quote especially speaks to you about finding balance? Why?

_____

_____

_____

_____

_____

_____

_____

_____

_____

© 2023 WHOLE PERSON ASSOCIATES, 101 WEST 2ND STREET, SUITE 203, DULUTH MN 55802 • 800-247-6789 • WHOLEPERSON.COM

Technology

Technology Overuse

Name _____

Date _____

The Technology Addiction Workbook — **TECHNOLOGY OVERUSE**

Technology Overuse Assessment
Introduction and Directions

Overuse means to use something too much ...
to use something excessively or too frequently.

People often overuse technology to mask problems and concerns and escape from reality.

The *Technology Overuse Assessment* contains 15 statements assessing how you might be using or overusing technology to cope with problem areas of your life.

Read each of the statements and decide whether or not it describes you. If it does describe you, circle the number in the YES column next to that item. If the statement does not describe you, circle the number in the NO column next to that item.

In the following example, the circled 2 indicates that the person completing this assessment believes that the statement describes them:

	YES	NO
I use technology to ...		
Deal with my stress	(2)	1
Help me cope with challenges	(2)	1

This is not a test. Since there are no right or wrong answers, do not spend too much time thinking about your answers. Be sure to respond to every statement. The purpose of this assessment is for YOU to learn more about YOU and your technology habits.

BE HONEST!

If you choose, no one else needs to see the results.

(Turn to the next page and begin.)

Technology Overuse Assessment

Name _____ Date _____

This will only be accurate if you respond honestly. No one else needs to see this if you choose.

	YES	NO

I use technology to ...

Deal with my stress	2	1
Help me cope with challenges	2	1
Escape negative feelings	2	1
Comfort me when I feel depressed	2	1
Relax and recharge myself	2	1

Stress TOTAL = _____

	YES	NO

I use technology to ...

Avoid being distracted	2	1
Close off the outside world	2	1
Escape from reality	2	1
Entertain me when I'm bored with life	2	1
Provide me with real-world information	2	1

Escape TOTAL = _____

	YES	NO

I use technology to ...

Connect with others from a distance	2	1
Socialize without actually meeting other people	2	1
Connect with others in the least scary way I can	2	1
Be my companion	2	1
Fulfill my social needs	2	1

Connection TOTAL = _____

Go to the next page for scoring assessment results, profile interpretation, and individual description.

Technology Overuse Assessment
Scoring Descriptions and Profile Interpretation

The assessment you completed on the previous page measures how you might be overusing technology to cope with various life issues.

In each of the sections on the previous page, count the numbers you circled. Put that number on the line marked TOTAL at the end of each section. Transfer your totals to the spaces below and place an X on the line representing your score:

Stress = _____ **Your use of technology to deal with stressful and challenging situations**

_____

5 = Low   **8 = Moderate**   **10 = High**

Escape = _____ **Your use of technology distracts you from life's reality**

_____

5 = Low   **8 = Moderate**   **10 = High**

Connection = _____ **Your use of technology to connect with others and build relationships**

_____

5 = Low   **8 = Moderate**   **10 = High**

Assessment Profile Interpretation

HIGH scores (9-20) indicate that you constantly use technology to cope with life issues.
MODERATE scores (7-8) indicate that you are using some technology to cope with life issues.
LOW scores (5-6) indicate that you are not using technology very often to cope with life issues.

Even one YES on a scale can suggest the overuse of technology. The HIGHER your score on the Technology Overuse Assessment, the more you use technology to overcome life issues.

Coping with Stress (Page 1)

Do you turn to technology when you get stressed? Many people addicted to technology find that they reach for one of their devices when they are experiencing stress. Rather than trying to cope with it, they attempt to escape their stress with technology. It would help if you learned basic techniques for coping with and managing stress without your devices. You will reduce the amount of anxiety you experience and live a full life not dependent on technology.

Review the last month. What coping techniques have you used? Find those techniques in the first column. In the second column, write about how it worked for you. In the third column, note the techniques you are willing to try and when you think they will help.

Stress-Management Techniques	How I Tried This and the Results	I Will Try This When …
Example: Breathing – *Take time to breathe. Take deep breaths in through your nose and breathe out through your mouth.*	*I tried it, and it worked well, especially when I couldn't fall asleep, but then I forgot to do it.*	
Breathing – Take time to breathe. Take deep breaths in through your nose and breathe out through your mouth.		
Physical Health – Be sure you exercise, sleep, and eat well.		
Relaxation – Find a quiet place to relax, do yoga, listen to soothing music, draw, participate in guided imagery, or write.		
Use Visualization – Visualize that you are not engaged with technology devices and are relaxed, happy, and safe.		

(Continued on the next page)

Coping with Stress (Page 2)

Review the last month. What coping techniques have you used? Find those techniques in the first column. In the second column, write about how it worked for you. In the third column, note the techniques you are willing to try and when you think they will help.

Stress-Management Techniques	How I Tried This and the Results	I Will Try This When ...
Distraction – Find productive, relaxing, and enjoyable ways to take your mind off your anxiety.		
Support – Confide in and talk with trusted friends and family or a therapist about your stress and anxiety.		
Spirituality – Finding purpose and meaning in life through introspection, meditation, and prayer.		
Journaling – Writing about your stress symptoms, triggers, and coping methods in a journal.		
Mindfulness – Staying present in the moment, noticing and being with your sensations, emotions, and thoughts.		
Meditation – Close your eyes and relax by focusing on counting your breaths. Clear your mind of all thoughts.		

The life of inner peace, being harmonious and without stress,
is the easiest type of existence.
~ Norman Vincent Peale

Think More Realistically

When you have stress in your life, your unrealistic inner dialogue can cause you to escape reality by engaging in technology.

Think and write about the various ways that you may be using technology to escape from stressful thoughts and how you can now explore ways to think realistically.

Examples of unrealistic thinking and how thoughts could be more realistic:

Unrealistic Thought: If I don't check my emails before bedtime, I may miss something from my boss!
More Realistic Thought: Nothing that comes in late at night is essential for my job.

Unrealistic Thought: If I'm not on Facebook, I could miss out on an important post.
More Realistic Thought: Nothing is so important on Facebook that it can't wait.

Unrealistic Thought: I can't make friends, so I have to interact with people through video games.
More Realistic Thought: I can make friends if I join some clubs and groups.

Unrealistic Thought #1: _____

_____

A More Realistic Thought: _____

_____

Unrealistic Thought #2: _____

_____

A More Realistic Thought: _____

_____

Unrealistic Thought #3: _____

_____

A More Realistic Thought: _____

_____

The great enemy of the truth is very often not the lie, deliberate, contrived, and dishonest, but the myth, persistent, persuasive, and unrealistic.
~ John F. Kennedy

Connected Online and Offline

People with a technology addiction often have many more friends online than offline. This is a self-fulfilling prophecy that keeps you overusing your technology devices.

Complete the table below to explore the level of your online connections.

People I Feel Connected to ONLINE (USE NAME CODE)	Our Relationship	Why I Feel Connected
Example: PGT	A stranger who I have never met.	I like to play video games with him because he is available 24/7. I don't know anything about him other than he likes to play.

Complete the table below to explore the level of your offline relationships.

People I Feel Connected to OFFLINE (USE NAME CODE)	Our Relationship	Why I Feel Connected
Example: LPE	A close relative.	She is always available to talk when I am feeling down on myself. All I need to do is call her, and she will come over to talk.

Which table was easier to complete, and why? _____

_____

_____

Thinking Like a Victim

Victim thinking can reflect a fearful, negative view of life, self, and the world due to technology overuse. The following checklist will allow you to explore how much you use victim thinking.

Place a check in the boxes that apply to you. Be honest!

- ☐ I can't make friends in the "real world."
- ☐ I have no control over how often I access my devices.
- ☐ I am liked on social media but not in real life.
- ☐ Things will never get better for me.
- ☐ I will never be able to reduce my interest in technology.
- ☐ I am sure I will always feel obsessed with my need to be on my devices.
- ☐ I will never be as popular in person as I am on social media.
- ☐ I can never succeed in reducing my need to game.
- ☐ I am different from other people because I can't make real friends.
- ☐ I don't think I overuse technology even though I spend a lot of time online.
- ☐ I know I lie a lot to cover up the time I spend on my devices.
- ☐ My tablet (or phone) is my only companion.
- ☐ I feel misunderstood because of my need to be on social media.
- ☐ I am ashamed of how much time I spend with technology, but I can't stop.
- ☐ I feel my life will be worse if I stop using my various devices so much.

Affirmations

Following are some affirmations you can say to yourself to feel less like a victim of technology overuse. Cut them out and put them in places where you will see them.

I am worthy just as I am!	I don't need so much technology!	I can reduce the use of my devices!
I am the master of my actions!	I am in the process of reducing my technology use!	My life with minimal technology still matters!
I can unplug!	I can be special without overusing technology!	I will put this addiction behind me!

Automatic Responses (Page 1)

Part of the problem for people who overuse their devices is that they respond automatically to bells and whistles, gaming noises, loud commercials, ring tones, and noisy alerts. You want to immediately see what the noise is about. Is someone texting me? Did I win a free game? Am I missing out on something? Is someone trying to reach me? Thus, any technology-related noise triggers your attention, and you automatically respond to it. These automatic responses can cloud your ability to concentrate, focus, and think clearly.

Formula to resist your urge to respond to technology automatically:

- Do not react to the trigger.

- Maintain focus on what you are currently doing or with whom you are talking.

- Mindfully notice the reaction being caused in your body and separate from it.

- Pause for a few seconds and take a couple of deep breaths.

- Monitor and change your negative thinking *(examples: something is wrong, I'm missing out on something, I might miss out on something important, they will think I don't care, etc.).*

List the types of technology you respond to automatically without thinking:

_____

_____

_____

After you receive a notification from one of your devices, go through the formula above.

As you receive the notification, what do you notice?

_____

_____

_____

Which device is it?_____

Automatic Responses (Page 2)

Do not react to the trigger. How did it feel to NOT automatically respond to the device that is calling to you?

_____

_____

_____

Maintain focus on what you are currently doing or with whom you are talking. How did it feel to NOT give in to the temptation to look at or respond to technology?

_____

_____

_____

Mindfully notice the reaction being caused in your body. What occurs in your body? Does your heart beat faster, do you jump, do you sweat, etc.?

_____

_____

_____

How can you notice it and then separate from it?

_____

_____

_____

Pause for a few seconds and take a couple of deep breaths. When you breathe deeply, you relax your body. How does it feel to relax rather than be on edge about the prompts?

_____

_____

_____

© 2023 WHOLE PERSON ASSOCIATES, 101 WEST 2ND STREET, SUITE 203, DULUTH MN 55802 • 800-247-6789 • WHOLEPERSON.COM

Automatic Responses (Page 3)

Monitor and change your negative thinking (something is wrong, I'm missing out on something, I might miss something important, they will think I don't care, etc.). What thoughts went through your mind?

_____

_____

_____

Were you able to dismiss them or make them more positive? What did you learn?

_____

_____

_____

Each time you rest in your brain's responsive mode,
it gets easier to come home to it again.
~ Rick Hanson

How does the above quotation apply to your automatic responses?

_____

_____

_____

_____

_____

_____

_____

_____

Your Stories about Unplugging

Unplugging does not mean never using technology. It means that every facet of our lives should not revolve around technology.

Write your technology-related stories in the space below.

My story about what my grandfather did without a computer.
My story about what I would do without a computer or other devices.
My story about what I do with technology that is significant.
My story about what I do with technology that is not very important.

No-Tech Leisure

Finding some no-tech alternatives to enjoy time spent without your devices is helpful. No-tech leisure activities might include playing a board game with someone, taking a walk, playing with a pet, going to the gym, playing or watching sports, reading a good book, going to a museum, seeing a good movie, writing poetry, going out for ice cream with someone you love, taking a leisurely drive in the country, etc.

Dig deep, and think of some no-tech, de-computerizing leisure activities you would enjoy. Write, draw, or doodle them below:

A no-tech leisure activity I might consider is …	A no-tech leisure activity I would like is …
A no-tech leisure activity I would love is …	A no-tech leisure activity I would do with someone whose company I enjoy is …

Join Something

Rather than using your devices 24/7, how about taking a class or joining a club that would have different people than those you already know? People with common interests doing activities that do not require your devices.

In the hexagons below, write down what you will consider joining. Be creative in your thinking.

Examples: A meditation or yoga class, or an amateur sports team.

What I Will Consider Joining

Habits

Creating a habit can be difficult, but it will help you overcome your excessive use of technology. A new non-tech habit will not happen immediately, but it will hold your interest over time.

Here are the steps in the habit-making process.

1. Start with small steps rather than going gung-ho and then quitting. Replace technology slowly and gradually. What are three small ways you will reduce your use of technology?

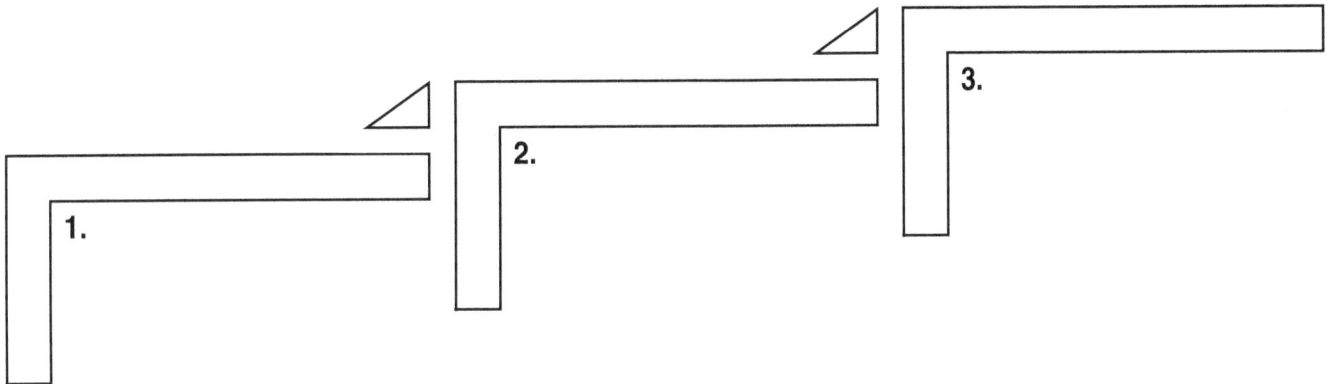

3.

2.

1.

2. Stay away from temptations that help feed your overuse of technology. What temptations will you stay away from? Write about them below:

Temptations	How I Will Stay Away From Them
Example: Gaming late at night.	*Keep all devices out of the bedroom.*

3. Replace old habits with new ones. Finding an alternative to your tech habit can help you replace it more easily. Write about your alternatives below:

Alternative	How I Will Use Them
Example: Reading	*I will read an actual book rather than use an electronic device.*

Making New Friends

Many people addicted to technology find it difficult to meet people in person. They would much rather meet people using an electronic device. When meeting people face-to-face, you need to be open to new experiences. Take it on as a project! Not everyone you meet will lead to a friendship, but you will learn from the experience and hopefully have some fun.

Below are some ways to meet new people. Which ones have you tried or want to try?

Ways to Meet New People	Tried It? Liked it or Not?	Not Tried it, But I Will Try It
Be Active in Your Neighborhood		
Become Involved in a Religious or Spiritual Group		
Cheer On a Sports Team		
Explore Neighborhood Attractions or Events		
Investigate Creative Galleries		
Join a Club or Organization		
Take a Class at a Local College		
Volunteer		
Walk a Dog, Yours or Someone Else's		
Other		

Which of the ways to meet new people sounds most appealing? _____

_____

_____

Justifications

People who overuse technology often justify their actions by thinking and saying that they are not overusing them. This only works against them and enables them to continue the overuse to the point of possible addiction.

What are some of the justifications you say to yourself? Some common justifications are listed below. Place a checkmark in front of the statements you use to justify your overuse of technology, and then take the other side of the argument and explain how you can UN-JUSTIFY each one.

☐ **Denial:** *"Technology is not a problem."*

_____

_____

☐ **Minimization:** *"I have already cut out plenty of my use of technology."*

_____

_____

☐ **Comparisons:** *"There are other addictions worse than technology."*

_____

_____

☐ **Defiance:** *"I would rather overuse technology than be alone and miserable."*

_____

_____

☐ **Rationalization:** *"I've got so many friends online, though."*

_____

_____

☐ **Lesser of Two Evils:** *"Better to have only online friends than no friends."*

_____

_____

☐ **Misinformation:** *"The use of technology can't hurt me."*

_____

_____

☐ **Taking Behavior out of Context:** *"Technology addiction is not a huge problem for me."*

_____

_____

☐ **Glorification:** *"People who use technology tend to be very successful."*

_____

_____

I'm Afraid of Rejection

People who overuse technology may be afraid of being rejected by someone. Meeting people means putting yourself out there and connecting, and that can be scary! It is especially intimidating if you're shy and introverted.

Personalize the following statements to explore your fear of rejection or insecurities.

I feel as if any rejection will haunt me forever.
I feel that when one person rejects me, it will prove that I'm unlikeable.
I feel that someone not wanting to be my friend will prove that I'm destined to be friendless.
Because of my fear of rejection, I prefer to interact online.

Some Healthy Ways to Handle Your Fear of Rejection

- Take a moment to check your assumptions. Just because someone isn't interested in talking or hanging out doesn't automatically mean they're rejecting you. They may be busy, distracted, or have other things going on.
- If someone seems as if they are not interested in being your friend, that does not mean they rejected you. Maybe they're having a bad day, misinterpreted something you said, or aren't looking for new friends.
- The other person may not be a nice person to anyone.
- You're not going to like everyone you meet, and everyone will not like you. Focus on the long-term goal of making quality connections rather than getting hung up on the ones that didn't work out.
- Keep rejection in perspective. Even though it never feels good if people aren't friendly or welcoming, it often has nothing to do with you. Instead of beating yourself up, give yourself credit for trying, and see what you have learned from the experience.
- Unplug. It's challenging to meet new people in any social situation if you're more interested in your phone than the people around you. Remove your headphones and put away your smartphone while in the checkout line. Making eye contact and exchanging small talk with strangers is great practice for making connections.

Keep Me on Track

Reducing your overuse of technology can be a difficult process. It often requires a team of offline people you trust to help you. These people can be friends, a mentor, siblings, relatives, someone at work, family members, etc.

Below, identify people you trust who can help keep you on track and help you remain accountable for reducing your overuse of technology.

People I Trust (USE NAME CODES)	Relationship to Me	How These People Can Help
HAN	A friend	He can jog with me when I get the urge to access social media.
MMA	A relative	She can suggest things for me to do rather than use my devices.

Be true to yourself and surround yourself with positive, supportive people.
~ Payal Kadakia

Need to Change Your Tech Habits?

Awareness is important in changing your technology overuse habits. It is important to think about when you would like to change them.

Below, list the day and the time when you most want to change your technology habits. Think about television, social media, the internet, video games, smartphone, tablet, etc.

Day of the Week_____

Times of the Day	My Use of Technology	Changes I Want to Make
Early Morning (5 am to 9 am)		
Morning (9 am to 12 Noon)		
Lunchtime (12 Noon to 2 pm)		
Late Afternoon (2 pm to 5 pm)		
Evening (5 pm to 9 pm)		
Night (9 am to Midnight)		
Late Night (Midnight to 5 am)		

The biggest competition is myself. I am not looking to follow
others or pull them down. I'm planning to test my own boundaries.
~ Rain

Quotes about Technology Overuse

*On the lines that follow each of the quotes, describe how the
quote speaks to you and how it applies to your life.*

So much of what we do every single day is the result
of habits that we have formed over time.
~ Joyce Meyer

_____

_____

The internet was supposed to homogenize everyone by connecting us all.
Instead, what it's allowed is silos of interest.
~ Seth Godin

_____

_____

The only way to avoid being miserable is not to have enough leisure
to wonder whether you are happy or not.
~ George Bernard Shaw

_____

_____

Being in control of your life and having realistic expectations about your
day-to-day challenges are the keys to stress management, which is perhaps
the most important ingredient to living a happy, healthy, and rewarding life.
~ Marilu Henner

_____

_____

Which quote especially speaks to you and your technology overuse? Why?

_____

_____

_____

_____

WholePerson

Whole Person Associates is the leading publisher of training
resources for professionals who empower people to create and
maintain healthy lifestyles. Our creative resources will help
you work effectively with your clients in the areas
of stress management, wellness promotion,
mental health, and life skills.

Please visit us at our website: **WholePerson.com**.
You can check out our entire line of products, place an order,
request our print catalog, and sign up for our monthly
special notifications.

Whole Person Associates
800-247-6789
Books@WholePerson.com

www.ingramcontent.com/pod-product-compliance
Lightning Source LLC
Chambersburg PA
CBHW082358270326
41935CB00013B/1678